# SMELL THE BOOK

# SMELL THE BOOK

## The Oral History of

**MARTY DiBERGI**

*with*

**DAVID ST. HUBBINS**
**DEREK SMALLS**
*and* **NIGEL TUFNEL**

*Foreword by* **DAVID BYRNE**

GALLERY BOOKS

New York   Amsterdam/Antwerp   London
Toronto   Sydney/Melbourne   New Delhi

# Contents

*Foreword by David Byrne* — vii

*Introduction* — 1

**CHAPTER 1:** Austerity Squatney — 5

**CHAPTER 2:** A Sound Is Born — 15

**CHAPTER 3:** The Flowering of Tap — 25

**CHAPTER 4:** The World's Loudest Band — 37

**CHAPTER 5:** The Wilderness Years — 45

**CHAPTER 6:** Faith, Fame, and Festivals — 53

**CHAPTER 7:** Rockin' in the Urn — 61

*Acknowledgments* — 65

# Foreword

## by David Byrne

As a somewhat secret Spinal Tap obsessive who follows the blogs, Reddit accounts, and social media rumors, much of this recent history of Tap is already familiar to me. But it's great to have the truth finally come out and the crazy rumors squashed. We didn't ever really believe they'd forgotten us. Or that the ceramics reportedly signed by St. Hubbins and spotted in a Swindon crafts shop were actually made by the reclusive one and only. Nonsense. Nor did we believe that Smalls thought *The Wicker Man* was a documentary and converted to the Anglican faith in a rural community in Scotland. He's always hated Scotland, so this all seemed a bit much to swallow. More rumors followed—an appearance on TMZ with Tufnel pushing a stroller. (Admittedly, it was revealed that it was filled with ale and not an infant.) The media campaigns must end! We have kept the faith. And now we are being rewarded.

The brilliant insights from Tap have become part of our culture—certainly part of musical culture; how many of us on the road have said "These go to eleven" or "Hello, Cleveland!" while lost in the bowels of some dank venue basement. Like in a Borges (or Phillip K. Dick) story, we wonder if the Gallagher brothers are reading from a script written by Tap. As if all of us who claim to be original and innovative yet are unknown even to ourselves are secretly reading from that illustrious manuscript.

And how great that the band, unlike another I won't mention, put aside their differences and animosities and gave the fans one last concert. And they still have it. The magic is still there . . . as is some of the hair. Look through this book. Here, like it or not (and I, for one, completely concur), is a glimpse, a prophecy, of our future, if we dare to bow down and admit it. Relax and let Tap lead the way.

—DB

# SMELL THE BOOK

# Introduction

One night in 1966, I wandered into a rock club called the Electric Banana in New York City's Greenwich Village. Don't look for it; it's not there anymore. But what I experienced that night, like a first kiss or a first case of food poisoning, made a lasting impression on me. That night, I heard a band that, for me, redefined the words "rock 'n' roll." I was completely blown away by their stage presence, their raw power—and their punctuality.

That band was Britain's now-legendary Spinal Tap. They have since earned a distinguished place in rock history as one of England's loudest bands. At the time, I never dreamed I would one day get the opportunity to make a documentary—an, if you will, rockumentary—about these musical legends. But in the fall of 1982, I learned that Tap was releasing a new album called *Smell the Glove* and planning what was to be their final tour, to promote the album. The news had me licking my cinematic chops. So I loaded my 16mm camera and set out to make rock and film history. The result was *This Is Spinal Tap*.

Although my film was met with critical praise and well over $100 in box office receipts, the band's three principals—guitarist and vocalist David St. Hubbins, guitarist and vocalist Nigel Tufnel, and bassist and vocalist Derek Smalls—were upset. They stopped speaking to me. They claimed that what I thought was an honest and loving portrait of the band was nothing more than a hatchet job. They felt I had placed way too much emphasis on the tour's mishaps. I was crestfallen.

Still, *This Is Spinal Tap* opened doors for me. After years of struggle, documenting weddings and bar mitzvahs and making commercials for La-Z-Boy recliners and Chuck Wagon dog food, I finally got an opportunity to direct a major motion picture: the sequel to an Academy Award–winning movie that had starred Dustin Hoffman and Meryl Streep. Sadly, *Kramer vs. Kramer vs. Godzilla* was met with a somewhat cool reception, and my career in feature films sank faster than a mobster in cement shoes.

After a long period in the wilderness, lost and broke, I entered the spiritual retreat of his holiness Baba Ram Das Boot and spent my days peacefully meditating and reading *Deadline Hollywood*. One day, after my yogic sound bath, I was sipping a spirulina smoothie and scrolling through TikTok when I came across something extraordinary: a video of two legendary country stars singing their version of Tap's famous anthem to women's derrieres, "Big Bottom."

The video was blowing up on social media. This, I would soon learn, piqued the interest of Hope Faith, the daughter of Spinal Tap's late manager, Ian Faith. She had inherited a contract from her father that called for one more Tap performance. What had for the longest time seemed like a worthless piece of paper now smelled of money. So, fifteen years after having acrimoniously split up, Tap was going to reunite for one last concert in New Orleans.

Call it fate, call it karma, call it an IRS notification informing me that I owed a sizable amount in back taxes—I saw this as a sign. So I decided to temporarily forgo enlightenment in pursuit of a filmic rebirth.

I contacted Hope and offered my services. She welcomed the idea. Still, I was worried about the band. In the decades since the original film's release, I had made several overtures to David, Nigel, and Derek in an effort to put the past behind us. Sadly, these overtures fell on deaf ears—not only because of their continuing animus toward me but because they were all battling hearing loss.

But thanks to the passage of time and significant advances in cochlear-implant technology, the guys agreed to give me a second chance. And I believe that *Spinal Tap II: The End Continues* will be the fitting capstone to my directorial oeuvre.

In addition to once again allowing me to chronicle their musical journey, Nigel, David, and Derek also agreed to collaborate with me on the book you are currently three pages into: the oral history of Spinal Tap. A few months ago, we convened for a conversation at the Village Recorders, the fabled L.A. studio where Fleetwood Mac's *Tusk*, Dr. Dre's *The Chronic*, and Whitney Houston's soundtrack to *The Bodyguard* were recorded. We now add the history of the legendary Spinal Tap to the Village's résumé.

But hey, enough of my preamblin'. Whaddya say? Let's historicalize!

—Marty DiBergi, Los Angeles, 2025

CHAPTER 1

# Austerity Squatney

*The future members of Spinal Tap were born into a postwar England struggling to rebuild itself after the Luftwaffe had reduced much of its capital city to rubble. But from this grim landscape, a revolution was about to emerge. A loud one.*

**MARTY DiBERGI:** Before we talk about the band and how you guys all found each other and started making music, I want to talk about you as individuals—your backgrounds, where you came from. Let's start with Nigel. Where were you born?

**NIGEL TUFNEL:** I was born in a section of London's East End, far, far, far east—E10, really—called Squatney.

**DAVID ST. HUBBINS:** E10. Not Eton. That's something else.

**NIGEL:** E10. That's a postal code. The Aldgate Pump, which has existed since medieval times, is a place in London that demarcates where the East End begins.

DEREK SMALLS: Or ends, depending on your point of view.

MARTY: And what was life like in the Tufnel home?

NIGEL: It was joyful, I suppose. We lived in Buckland Road first, and my dad had the same job as my granddad.

MARTY: Which was?

NIGEL: They made wind socks.

MARTY: You mean the things at the airports that tell you which way the wind is blowing?

NIGEL: Yeah.

DAVID: Top-line. They were the best wind socks.

NIGEL: Yeah. They were handsewn, as they did things then. My mum was a houseperson, as they called it.

MARTY: Did she wash the socks?

NIGEL: No, but on occasion she darned them.

MARTY: Interesting.

NIGEL: It was quite a happy home. My dad was quite musical. My mum was a singer, but not a professional singer. And my granddad was the first to give me a used guitar, a Harmony Sovereign. It was beaten up a bit, but I was thrilled. I think I was about twelve.

MARTY: Did you have brothers and sisters?

NIGEL: I had a brother.

MARTY: And what happened to him?

NIGEL: Nothing.

MARTY: You put it in past tense and I just assumed that he had passed away.

NIGEL: Oh, no. He's still alive, but we don't talk.

MARTY: There's some bad blood there?

NIGEL: Yes. There's a name for it.

DEREK: Bad blood.

NIGEL: No, another name.

DAVID: Brother-shunting.

MARTY: Do you want to talk a little about what happened that caused you not to talk to each other?

NIGEL: No.

MARTY: Was he an older brother or a younger brother?

NIGEL: I don't remember.

DAVID: I've pressed him on this. He's not going to talk. I vaguely remember his brother.

MARTY: What was his name?

NIGEL: Now you've got me under the gun. It was either Philip . . .

DAVID: Or Kevin . . .

NIGEL: Or Charles.

DAVID: I remember he had a rash. Some kind of strawberry birthmark.

MARTY: But you have no idea what happened to him.

NIGEL: Not off the top of my head.

**DEREK:** Or any other part of your head.

**MARTY:** Okay. So, David, where were you born?

**DAVID:** I was born in the same hospital he was, in Squatney. I lived right 'round the corner.

**MARTY:** So you lived in the same neighborhood?

**NIGEL:** I was in Buckland Road, and he was . . .

**DAVID:** In Can Street.

**MARTY:** How old were you when you first met each other?

**NIGEL:** It's hard to remember exactly.

**MARTY:** Well, I'm assuming that if you can't remember who your brother was, it's probably hard to remember the exact age you were.

**NIGEL:** But that's a different thing. That's a family thing.

**DAVID:** He's blocking. And there was—maybe you're not familiar with this in the United States—a plague of unexploded bombs that were being uncovered as they pushed the rubble from World War II aside.

**MARTY:** From the Blitzkrieg. That must have left everyone traumatized.

**NIGEL:** Especially in the East End. If you'd go to East India Dock Road, you were seeing rubble still.

**MARTY:** You're not talking about Barney Rubble from *The Flintstones*.

**DAVID:** No, I never met him. *Admired* him. Anyway, we heard that there was an unexploded bomb right 'round the corner.

NIGEL: The word got out in our neighborhood.

DAVID: And it was like, "We're having that." So we went over to look at it, and that's the first time I laid eyes on Nigel. We were six.

MARTY: And they were able to defuse that bomb?

DAVID: Well, it turned out it was a water tank.

NIGEL: It was from someone's house or something. It looked enough like a bomb that they brought in the experts. But I saw David, and he saw me, and there was just this moment of . . .

DAVID: "Where are you from?" He says, "I live over here." And I said, "I live over there." And we were pointing almost in the same direction.

NIGEL: But we went to different schools. I was at Bunsell Street Primary School.

DAVID: I was at Sacred Sacrament. My mum was a big Catholic.

MARTY: Religious?

DAVID: No, five foot ten.

MARTY: What was life like in the St. Hubbins home?

DAVID: It was difficult because my parents didn't really care for each other, old Ivor and Ruby. There were a lot of rows. And us kids, we would just kind of flinch and crouch.

MARTY: You had brothers and sisters?

DAVID: One sister.

**MARTY:** And did you know her name?

**DAVID:** I do. It's Sheila.

**MARTY:** And where is Sheila?

**DAVID:** Sheila's gone to Australia. All women there are called Sheila.

**DEREK:** It's a common noun there.

**DAVID:** Yeah. So she figured she'd fit right in.

**MARTY:** You said there was a lot of fighting between your mom and dad.

**DAVID:** Constantly.

**MARTY:** Do you remember what they were fighting about?

**NIGEL:** Yeah, it had something to do with her putting the mustard in the wrong place on the table.

**DAVID:** Oh, yeah, the mustard fights were legendary.

**NIGEL:** I remember the first time going over to David's and there was a row going on. So, a lot of those times, he'd come over to my house, where things were calm.

**MARTY:** What did your dad do for a living?

**DAVID:** He ran a luggage-repair shop just outside Squatney.

**NIGEL:** But most of the time he was out on the road.

**DAVID:** He had this little van and he would travel around to all of the resort areas, all the coastal resorts. Even though his name was Ivor, he called himself Johnny on the Spot. He would park outside the hotels and he would say to people either coming or going, "I see you have broken your luggage, let's do something about it."

NIGEL: Usually, it was handles. Handles break a lot.

MARTY: And that was a good business, waiting outside hotels hoping that someone would turn up with broken luggage?

DAVID: Not really. I think he just liked getting out of the house and away from Ruby. Eventually, Ruby made it official and got away from him.

MARTY: They got divorced?

DAVID: Yeah.

MARTY: How old were you?

DAVID: Fifteen. Right around the time I started playing with this geezer.

NIGEL: We'd go to the clubs. The Ealing Club and the Marquee. The Flamingo was a famous place. We'd see people play and that would then affect how we played.

DAVID: He had all the records.

MARTY: Like 45s?

NIGEL: Well, they were 78s. Ten-inch records from my granddad and dad.

MARTY: I'm going to dive further into how you guys first started playing together. But before we do that, I want to turn to Derek.

DEREK: You turned well.

**MARTY:** Yes, I physically turned to you, and now I'm looking at you. Derek, where were you born?

**DEREK:** And I'm turning to you to answer.

**DAVID:** Letting the action suit the words.

**DEREK:** I was born in the West Midlands, out in the countryside.

**MARTY:** What did your father do?

**DEREK:** In those days, there was a very good business in sanitizing telephones. People were worried about the germs. Word had gotten out.

**MARTY:** And germs had gotten out.

**DEREK:** The germs had gotten out. Chasing the words, really, or vice versa. So my dad, Duff, had a little truck that he'd drive about the countryside—and, later on, in the smaller cities in the West Midlands. His business was called SaniFone. When I was three or four, I started riding with him and learning the trade. So even up to this day, if you had a telephone that needed sanitizing, I could do it.

**MARTY:** Well, it's interesting, because I guess in those days it was all landlines. Now it's cell phones. Is there still a business to sanitize cell phones?

**DEREK:** It's interesting you ask. I've often thought that if my dad had lived long enough, he'd have a phone-sanitizing app and be a millionaire.

**MARTY:** You mean an app in the phone that would allow the phone to sanitize itself?

**DEREK:** Sanitize itself.

**MARTY:** Like an internal sanitizer.

**DEREK:** Exactly.

**MARTY:** And you said your dad's name was Duff?

**DEREK:** Correct.

**DAVID:** Is that short for anything?

**DEREK:** Duffman.

**MARTY:** Did you have brothers and sisters?

**DEREK:** No, only child.

**MARTY:** What were things like in the Smalls home?

**NIGEL:** Strained.

**MARTY:** Your mom and dad didn't get along?

**DEREK:** No. Rosa was a frustrated singer. When I was four, she left us to join a musical quartet called the Hotten Totties. She was an alto in the Hotten Totties.

**MARTY:** So that's where you get your deep voice.

**DEREK:** I imagine so. They were touring much of the year. I rarely saw her.

**DAVID:** What kind of music did they do?

**DEREK:** It was sort of ragtime, but forties ragtime. So more rag than time.

**MARTY:** Did your dad ever get remarried?

**DEREK:** He never did. He was married to his business. To him it was not just a business, it was a calling. *Literally* a calling.

**N**ow would be a good time for me to fill you in about my own humble beginnings. I was born Martin Bernardi on March 5, 1947. We lived in a predominantly Italian and Jewish neighborhood in the Bronx.

My father, Anthony Bernardi, ran a hero shop on Arthur Avenue. My mother, Sylvia, was Jewish and a homemaker with a great singing voice. Growing up, our apartment was filled with the sounds of Ella Fitzgerald, Sarah Vaughan, and Nina Simone. When rock 'n' roll made the scene, my mother embraced it. She loved Buddy Holly, Little Richard, and Chuck Berry. Lawrence Welk gave her migraines.

When I was just seven years old, my parents took me and my sister, Rosalie, to the local Loews movie theater to see Prince Valiant. From the moment I saw Robert Wagner in his pageboy haircut, I knew what I wanted to be. No, not a gay man with a chain-mail fetish, but a filmmaker.

Though my father was Italian, I was raised as a Jew, and for my bar mitzvah, my parents got me an 8mm film camera. From that moment on, there was no stopping me. I filmed everything in sight, from a butterfly landing on a flower to my father farting as he fell asleep watching The Ed Sullivan Show. Since the camera had no sound, you couldn't hear the farts. But trust me, they were not silent, just deadly.

# CHAPTER 2

# A Sound Is Born

*Out of the emptiness: salvation! The early days of the Tufnel–St. Hubbins musical alliance provided a pathway out of hardship and dead-end lives spent mending wind socks and repairing luggage. But the pathway was anything but straightforward.*

**MARTY:** When did you first start making music together?

**DAVID:** It was around the time that my folks broke up, age fourteen or maybe fifteen.

**NIGEL:** He was spending more and more time at my place.

**DAVID:** He had a guitar with all six strings. I had a four-string tenor.

**NIGEL:** We would listen to records for hours. Blues records. Blind Bubba Cheeks was one. Lonnie Johnson, Alexis Korner, people like that.

**DAVID:** Also, domestic skiffle like Lonnie Donegan.

**NIGEL:** Yes. He was huge. And then we eventually started figuring out things from the records.

**DAVID:** There was one tune called "Hoot Hoot." That was the only lyric, "Hoot hoot." But the playing was fucking amazing.

**MARTY:** So when did you guys start doing it officially? Where did you perform first?

**NIGEL:** In the streets. Outside of a Tube station. You put a hat down or whatever.

**MARTY:** Did you make any money?

**DAVID:** Enough to buy a new hat.

**NIGEL:** If you're lucky.

**MARTY:** Were you doing your own music?

**NIGEL:** No, we did mostly covers.

**DAVID:** Well, all covers.

**NIGEL:** When I said "mostly," I meant "all."

**MARTY:** What was your first original song?

**DAVID:** "All the Way Home."

**NIGEL:** Yeah. And that has skiffle roots.

**MARTY:** And when was the first time you were hired to play in a club?

**NIGEL:** Well, you didn't get paid, but you could go to the clubs. The Half Moon in Putney, places like that. You would just show up. And then it was a string of people playing. It would go on all night.

**DAVID:** I do recall that at one point, we each had a skiffle band. You were in a group called the Lovely Lads. And I was with the Creatures.

**MARTY:** So the first official group that you were in was not with each other?

**DAVID:** There was some other connection. I don't even remember who it was. Was it Coy Devon?

**NIGEL:** No. There was this chap called Bumby.

**DAVID:** Bumby, right.

**NIGEL:** He played . . . It wasn't a real bass, it was a string and a washtub. And you could bend this little broomstick back, and it would be the notes. Bumby could play that.

**MARTY:** So Bumby was like the glue between you guys.

**DEREK:** I find that people who play bass are often the glue.

**MARTY:** So, it was you two and Bumby?

**DAVID:** Yeah, that was the beginning of the Originals.

**MARTY:** So the Originals was the three of you. Who else was in the Originals?

**NIGEL:** Well, Bumby was in it for a little bit, and then he left. He went to Richmond and joined some other group. The important thing was to have a name: the Originals, in our case.

**MARTY:** And that's a great name, because it seems like you were the first to do what you did.

**DAVID:** Except that we weren't. There was already a group called the Originals.

NIGEL: Also in the East End.

DAVID: So we changed our name.

MARTY: To what?

DAVID: The New Originals. But then, the original Originals broke up.

MARTY: So did you go back to being the Originals?

DAVID: No, we became the Regulars.

MARTY: Do you remember your first gig as the Regulars?

DAVID: Yeah. It was the Queen's Lips.

NIGEL: It was a pub, basically.

DAVID: But they had a stage.

NIGEL: Yeah. We got two pounds or something.

MARTY: Then, from there, I understand, you were hired to be part of the Johnny Goodshow Revue?

DAVID: Yeah. That was fluky, wasn't it? Johnny Goodshow was not his real name. It was just a stage name. He was quite a man about town.

MARTY: He probably thought if he called himself Goodshow, it would be a way of letting people know they'd be in for a good time. What was his real name?

DAVID: Billy Goodshow.

NIGEL: He was a hustler.

MARTY: And you did a tour with him?

DAVID: Yeah. We played the seaside circuit. I knew all those venues from my dad.

**MARTY:** From fixing the handles on suitcases.

**DAVID:** Yeah.

**NIGEL:** I remember Blackpool the best, because there was the deepest sadness about that place.

**DAVID:** There was one club, the Waves. It was actually a ballroom from the days when they would have dancing and all that. We played this immense ballroom to an audience of about ten.

**MARTY:** That *is* sad.

**DAVID:** Then we played in a pub near the Waves called the Bucket. Which is still there. It's now called the Bucket and Pail.

**MARTY:** That seems redundant.

**DAVID:** I guess you could say that.

**DEREK:** He just did.

**DAVID:** Anyway, that's when we first met Stumpy Pepys.

**NIGEL:** Yeah, for the first time.

**DAVID:** That's what I said.

**NIGEL:** I said it, too.

**DAVID:** At that time, Stumpy was drumming for the Leslie Cheswick Soul Explosion.

**NIGEL:** He was good, Stumpy was.

**DAVID:** Great drummer.

**MARTY:** How did he get the name Stumpy?

**DAVID:** I don't know. I've never seen him naked, so who knows?

NIGEL: I was afraid to ask, frankly, because I thought it was you-know-what.

DAVID: You were afraid that if you said, "Why do they call you Stumpy?" he'd say, "Well, it's because of little stumpy here." Anyway, Stumpy joined us, and since Bumby had left music to become an ornithologist, it was only the three of us. Until we found a bass player named Ronnie Pudding.

DAVID: He was with a group called Cheap Dates.

NIGEL: Ronnie was a good songwriter.

DAVID: And he could arrange things. He did the string arrangement for "Rainy Day Sun."

NIGEL: Very talented.

MARTY: And at that point you called yourselves what?

DAVID: The Thamesmen. We did "Gimme Some Money" and we got some traction with it. It actually got played a bit. When we first heard it on the radio, it was kind of amazing.

NIGEL: At first, we thought there was something wrong with the radio.

DAVID: So Nigel hit it.

NIGEL: But our song kept playing, so . . .

MARTY: Is that when you left England?

DAVID: Yeah. We toured the Benelux nations.

NIGEL: Someone knew someone. It's always that. Someone would say, "I know someone in Amsterdam or Bruges or someplace, and you should go there." And we would just pack up and go.

MARTY: And how long were you in Amsterdam?

DAVID: Three weeks. We played a lot of gigs.

NIGEL: The Belgian people loved us. And there were some nice female people in Belgium as well.

DAVID: There still might be.

NIGEL: True. But they're probably dead.

MARTY: And that's when you picked up a keyboard player?

DAVID: Jan Van Der Kvelk.

NIGEL: Yeah. He had one of those funny symbols over one of the letters.

DAVID: Yeah. What are those?

NIGEL: They're not umlauts. They're something else.

DAVID: Omelets.

NIGEL: He was a magical player.

MARTY: It seems like you had a good run in the Benelux nations. But when you left, you didn't take Van Der Kvelk?

DAVID: No, we did. That's when we started calling ourselves the Dutchmen. Because of Jan being Dutch and all. But he didn't stay long because "Gimme Some Money" started charting again. So we switched back to the Thamesmen. But then that faded. And we were kind of at sea.

NIGEL: Not literally.

DAVID: No, not in a boat or anything.

MARTY: You were lost.

DAVID: You could say that.

**DEREK:** He just did.

**MARTY:** At this point, you went through a lot of changes. I'm looking at your history. It says that you performed as the Rave Breakers, Hellcats, Flamin' Daemons, Shiners, Mondos, the Doppel Gang, the Peoples, Loose Lips, Waffles, Hot Waffles, Silver Service, the Mud Below, and the Tufnel–St. Hubbins Group.

**NIGEL:** But it didn't fool the people.

**MARTY:** Because it was always the same people with different names?

**DAVID:** Right. But when we became the Tufnel–St. Hubbins Group, that was really sort of a turning point. We started piling on the instruments. Denny Upham and Dickie Lane joined the group. We added horns, Jimmy Adams and Geoff Clovington. And had two female backup singers.

**NIGEL:** Lhasa Apso . . .

**DAVID:** And Julie Scrubbs-Martin. Lhasa was my first serious girlfriend. Beautiful girl. She had an adorable lateral lisp. But now we had, like, nine people on the stage. And it wasn't really working the way we thought it would.

**MARTY:** Was that when you connected with that record executive?

**NIGEL:** Well, he wasn't a record executive at the time. He was a harp player, harmonica player. Little Danny Schindler.

**DAVID:** He played with the Schvegman-Hayman-Kvelkman Blues Band.

**NIGEL:** He was what, four seven?

**DAVID:** Dripping wet.

**MARTY:** Well, that wouldn't affect his height.

**DAVID:** Not technically, no.

**NIGEL:** He was quite a good harp player. But he was so short. They didn't make microphone stands at that time that could go that low. So for a while, we were calling him Boxy, because he had to stand on a box.

**DAVID:** He was an Orthodox Jew, never played on Saturday.

**NIGEL:** Yeah. When he played he'd tuck his payos under his hat.

**DAVID:** And when he signed with CPR Records, his group was called Talmud.

**MARTY:** He was really leaning into his Jewishness.

**NIGEL:** He played klezmer for many years.

**DAVID:** Heavy klezmer.

**NIGEL:** Electrified klezmer.

**DEREK:** Wasn't he known then as Davening Danny Schindler?

**DAVID:** It was Davenin' Danny Schindler, with an apostrophe.

**NIGEL:** And on one of the album covers, the picture was him as David, the famous David from the Bible, with that sling thing.

**DEREK:** And he had the harmonica at the end of the sling.

**MARTY:** He was going to hit Goliath with the harmonica?

**DEREK:** It was implied.

**NIGEL:** It was a famous album cover.

**Y**ou're probably wondering, or maybe you weren't, where I was developmentally at this point.

My first film was an eight-minute short called Make-Out at the Feast. It was about two teenagers, played by my sister and her boyfriend, who get caught making out behind a statue of the Virgin Mary during the Feast of San Gennaro. Because it included a flash of my sister's breast, showings of the film became a staple at neighborhood parties.

After graduating from Evander Childs High School, I applied to the film schools at NYU, USC, and UCLA. I submitted Make-Out at the Feast as a calling card. Unfortunately, they, along with fourteen other colleges, rejected me. I did, however, get accepted into the Ed Wood School of Cinematic Arts. There I came under the tutelage of Mr. Ed Wood himself, the master filmmaker behind Plan 9 from Outer Space. It was from Mr. Wood that I learned how to dangle a miniature flying saucer on a string to create the illusion of a spacecraft hurtling through the cosmos. Although I never found the opportunity to use this technique in my future filmic endeavors, it served me well as a life lesson. Whenever I was feeling that my directorial career was hanging by a thread, somewhere in the nether regions of my brain I knew I could still fly. And fly I did. Into the waiting arms of Spinal Tap.

## CHAPTER 3

# The Flowering of Tap

As the mid-sixties dawned, so, too, did a new consciousness among young people. For David St. Hubbins and Nigel Tufnel, the mid-sixties also dawned, but consciousness? Not so much. However, their bassist, Ronnie Pudding, came up with "(Listen to the) Flower People," a song that reflected the times, a song with its finger on the zeitgeist, a song that would forever change the trajectory of the band newly renamed Spinal Tap. And it was with Ronnie's abrupt departure from Tap that a new bassist entered the picture: one Derek Smalls.

**MARTY:** The first gig you played as Spinal Tap was at—

**DAVID:** At the Music Membrane.

**NIGEL:** It was near Leicester Square.

**MARTY:** Were you playing at the time what has come to be known as heavy metal?

**DAVID:** We sort of were, but then all of a sudden, everyone was talking about San Francisco.

**MARTY:** You mean like Scott McKenzie singing, "If you're going to San Francisco, be sure to wear some flowers in your hair"?

**DAVID:** Yeah, and there were also the Flower Pot Men and all these other groups. So we said, "Let's see if we can throw something together." So we came up with "(Listen to the) Flower People."

**MARTY:** So your first big hit wasn't heavy metal?

**DAVID:** Right. We were tempted *not* to call ourselves Spinal Tap.

**MARTY:** Because the idea of a spinal tap, which is an invasive medical procedure, is kind of at odds with this idea of flower power.

**DEREK:** A spinal tap is painful, that's really what you're saying.

**MARTY:** I am saying that.

**DEREK:** Flowers aren't painful.

**MARTY:** Not if used properly.

**DAVID:** Well, stick a rose in somebody's eye, that's going to hurt.

**MARTY:** So Ronnie Pudding recorded "Flower People" with you. But then he wasn't with the band when the song hit.

**DAVID:** Right, he was a bit of an egomaniac. He had written quite a bit of "Flower People." We all helped, but he did the most. And his head became enormous. We've always been very democratic, but he wanted to be the autocrat.

MARTY: So what happened to him after that?

DAVID: He formed Pudding People.

NIGEL: Which went nowhere.

DAVID: And he put out an album called *I Am the Music.*

NIGEL: And judging from the sales, the public said, "No, you aren't."

DAVID: So when Mr. Pudding was relegated to the back of the fridge, we met our current bass player. Our final bass player: Mr. Derek Smalls.

DEREK: Thank you very much.

MARTY: And what had you been doing up 'til that point?

DEREK: I was in this band called Mileage, which was sort of dance rock. Which wasn't a thing in those days. And then I joined this really pathbreaking group called Skaface, which was the only all-white ska band. Which got us in a lot of trouble.

MARTY: For, like, cultural appropriation?

DEREK: Yeah. The Skaface Riots were fairly notorious, especially in the North of England.

DAVID: We rescued him from that wasp's nest.

MARTY: People resented the fact that you were all-white?

DEREK: Yeah. And I think we did, too, in a way.

MARTY: You resented yourself?

DEREK: Well, I think we wished that one of us was Black.

MARTY: So "Flower People" becomes a hit. And you play the States, with Derek playing when you appeared on *Jamboreebop*.

**DEREK:** I was finger-syncing Ronnie's part. It wouldn't have been what I played.

**DAVID:** But you know what he did? When Derek came in, he learned every tune within days. And then, as we went on touring, we'd noticed that he was subtly changing all the older stuff.

**DEREK:** Making it my own.

**DAVID:** We thought, "Great, we have a bass player who's actually contributing."

**DEREK:** I'm a fast study. Same way I learned to sanitize phones, like this. [Snaps fingers.]

**MARTY:** So you essentially sanitized Ronnie Pudding's tracks.

**DAVID:** You debugged them.

**DEREK:** Yeah.

**MARTY:** I also noticed that when you did "Flower People" on *Jamboreebop* that there was a new drummer.

**DAVID:** Right, it was Stumpy Joe Childs. The reason we called him Stumpy Joe was—I forget why. Probably the same reason I forget why we called Stumpy Stumpy. The original Stumpy was great, but sadly he passed away shortly before we recorded "Flower People."

**MARTY:** And it's well known that he died in a bizarre gardening accident.

**DAVID:** Yeah.

**MARTY:** Do we have any particulars on that?

NIGEL: I think it's the vagueness that haunts us, because we don't know how it happened.

DEREK: We don't even know what tool he was using.

NIGEL: That's what I mean. If we knew, let's say if it was a spade or a hoe or whatever, it would be worse in some way.

DEREK: But it would be closure.

MARTY: How would that be closure?

NIGEL: Because then you have the full story in your mind. You know what happened. Right now it's "What do you mean, 'bizarre'? What happened?" "Don't really know." So it just lingers on.

DAVID: So sad.

MARTY: So how did you find his successor, Stumpy Joe?

DAVID: He was playing with a group called . . . Wool Cave?

NIGEL: Yeah. They didn't tune up.

DAVID: No.

NIGEL: That was considered to be—they don't use this term now—but you'd say, "Oh, he's a nancy boy if he tunes up." It was basically saying, "That's a poofter thing, to tune up." Which, again, they wouldn't say now. Although I just did say it.

DAVID: Stumpy Joe was the best part of Wool Cave.

NIGEL: Very powerful drummer.

MARTY: And he stayed with you for quite a while. He played on *Brainhammer, Blood to Let, Nerve Damage, Intravenus de Milo*.

DAVID: And he made the first tour of America with us. We played Boston, New York . . .

NIGEL: Boston again.

DAVID: Boston again, then Chicago.

NIGEL: Then Boston.

MARTY: And you were touring with your album *Listen to the Flower People*?

DAVID: In the States, it was called *Spinal Tap Sings "Listen to the Flower People" and Other Favorites*.

MARTY: What were some of the other favorites?

DEREK: There was a song called "Moon Base." I cowrote it with a girl I was with at the time. It was kind of an LSD thing where humans were setting up bases on the moon and playing rock 'n' roll.

DAVID: And there was one tune we had called "The Spelunker." It was about cave exploration.

NIGEL: It was supposed to be a mysterious sort of thing, because when people go down into caves, you're going into darkness.

DEREK: And do you know what changes that people don't think about? Gravity. The deeper you go in a cave, the heavier you are. So it's no place to be when you're on a diet.

MARTY: So it's the opposite of going into space, where you lose gravity.

DEREK: You get to the center of the Earth and you weigh, like, a thousand pounds.

DAVID: Arthur C. Clarke thought that at the center of the Earth, there's a diamond. Fucking lunatic.

DEREK: It's so hot down there. Wouldn't the diamonds melt?

DAVID: It's not hot, it's just stuffy.

NIGEL: In books I've read—*Journey to the Center of the Earth*, *At the Earth's Core* by Edgar Rice Burroughs—they have different people living there.

DEREK: Did he have Tarzan living at the center of the Earth?

NIGEL: No.

MARTY: But Burroughs was suggesting that there were people living at the center of the Earth?

NIGEL: Yes.

MARTY: Do you think there are?

NIGEL: I don't know, I've never been there.

DEREK: There are no people living at the center of the Earth.

NIGEL: And you've been there, I suppose?

DEREK: No. But why would they be living there? When they could be living anywhere.

NIGEL: Maybe they're not aware of their options.

MARTY: I don't know if we're going to solve this today.

DAVID: Yeah.

MARTY: Tell me about your producer at that time, Glyn Hampton-Cross.

NIGEL: He was a very gifted guy. He could hear parts that we couldn't hear.

**DAVID:** He had the strangest habit. Sometimes he would start speaking to you like, "Th— sc— crt." I'd say, "What are you doing?" And he said, "I'm leaving out the vowels."

**MARTY:** He would talk without using vowels?

**DAVID:** Yeah. So, in saying, like, "Where did I leave the car?" he'd say, "Wh— d— th— cr?" I don't know why he would do it.

**NIGEL:** He was a prodigy. He went to the Royal Academy of Music and he did the same thing with music. If he was singing a song, he would skip notes. He was so fast that, sometimes, he would skip right to the end.

**DAVID:** He once sang a piece, all rests.

**MARTY:** Sounds like a tough record producer to work with, one that doesn't use vowels and skips notes.

**DAVID:** He had his quirks.

**MARTY:** It sounds like if he were producing today, he would be into that sound thing where you are close to the microphone and—what's that called?

**DAVID:** ASMR.

**DEREK:** What is that?

**NIGEL:** Is that an assisted-living thing?

**MARTY:** No, it's like when you, like, rub flannel on five-o'clock shadow very close to the mic.

**DAVID:** It's supposed to be comforting. I find it annoyingly pointless.

# THE FLOWERING OF TAP

MARTY: So *Flower People* goes gold. Then the follow-up album, *We Are All Flower People*, from what I remember, didn't do as well.

DAVID: We stayed at the dance too long.

NIGEL: It's like that old saying that my granddad used to say, "Ride the horse until he poos." It's that old cliché.

MARTY: Never heard that one.

NIGEL: It's well known.

DAVID: The big problem with *We Are All Flower People* was that Denny Upham, our keyboard player at the time, sort of took over and got very experimental, pulling all this weird crap. There'd be a boogie-woogie riff and he'd reach into the piano where the strings are and start rubbing them.

MARTY: So you fired him?

DAVID: Yeah, we had to let him go. Then we went on as a four-piece for a while, opening for Matchstick Men.

MARTY: And then you finally made a big splash at the Electric Zoo.

DAVID: Right, in North London.

DEREK: Hampstead.

NIGEL: No, it was closer to Islington.

DAVID: Wherever it was, it's not there anymore.

MARTY: And the next album you came out with was *Silent but Deadly?*

DAVID: Yes. We recorded that live at the Zoo.

MARTY: And, Nigel, is that where you started doing your famous solos?

NIGEL: Yeah, that became a signature thing for a bit. People seemed to like it.

DAVID: Until they started to go on a bit too long.

MARTY: What would you say was your longest solo?

NIGEL: Oh, I did ones that were hours long.

MARTY: And you could hold the audience for that long?

NIGEL: No.

DEREK: You didn't hold your fellow band members that long.

NIGEL: No. At a certain point, they'd leave the stage.

MARTY: And do what?

DEREK: I'd usually have a dinner reservation nearby.

DAVID: Sometimes I'd get my waxing done.

NIGEL: So I cut them down a bit.

MARTY: I've noticed that you often incorporate classical elements into your playing.

NIGEL: Well, I didn't study classical music per se—

DEREK: You didn't study it at all.

NIGEL: That's true. It's an unconscious thing. I listen to Beethoven and Mozart, Bach and Corelli. Telemann, Shostakovich, whoever. And it just sort of goes into my head, rumbles about a bit, and then just comes out.

**MARTY:** So what you're saying is, a healthy diet of classical music keeps you regular.

**NIGEL:** I don't know what that means, but it sounds right.

**I**, too, traveled a long and winding road to artistic fulfillment. Upon my graduation from the Ed Wood School of Cinematic Arts, I was prepared to enter the world of filmmaking. I immediately landed an unpaid job as an assistant production assistant on an industrial film that celebrated the topsy-turvy world of meatpacking. During the shoot, I met the film's producer, Manny Endevers, who was impressed with my ability to deliver six coffees, all with different amounts of cream, sugar, and artificial sweeteners, to individual crew members, always remembering who got what. He said I had a bright future and offered me a lifelong job as production assistant. Although I would remain unpaid, it offered me job security. So I decided to hitch my wagon to Manny and embraced the ever-unpredictable world of industrials. Then one day, while working on a film about coin-operated vibrating beds, it hit me: I was trapped in a career cul-de-sac.

So I thanked Manny for all he had done for me and bade him farewell. I then proceeded to dust off my 8mm camera and offer up my services to anyone who needed a wedding, a christening, a bar mitzvah, or a bris documented. One day, while shooting Artie Berns's bar mitzvah, I met a wealthy furrier named Murray Gussoff. He asked me if I was interested in directing a commercial for a chain of stores he owned called Murray's Minks. I jumped at the chance. And before I knew it, I became the go-to guy for local-TV spots. I shot commercials for Carmine's Cleaners, Eddie & Freddy "the Bagel Boys," and Salvatore's Pizza Parlor and Shoe Repair, where you could enjoy a slice while waiting for a resole.

I was well on my way to browner pastures.

## CHAPTER 4

# The World's Loudest Band

The early seventies Spinal Tap lineup—*David, Nigel, Derek, and Stumpy Joe*—crisscrossed the globe on the backs of Brainhammer, Blood to Let, Nerve Damage, Intravenus DeMilo, *and the concept album* The Sun Never Sweats, *for which they were joined by a new keyboard player, Ross MacLochness.*

*The endless cycle of album-tour-album-tour was not without its casualties. During the recording of* The Sun Never Sweats, *Eric "Stumpy Joe" Childs was found dead. To anyone who has seen my documentary* This Is Spinal Tap, *the story is familiar: Stumpy Joe choked on vomit, but not his own. Because a forensic test for vomit hadn't yet been developed, it wasn't possible to determine whose vomit it was. To this day, the case remains unsolved.*

*However, I understand that crime labs around the world are developing technologies that shall assist the police and future victims of vomit-choking.*

MARTY: Let's talk about *The Sun Never Sweats*. That's when you hired Ross MacLochness.

DAVID: Yes. And having lost Stumpy Joe, Peter "James" Bond came in to play on most of that.

MARTY: How did you find Ross MacLochness?

DAVID: Ross was with a Scottish band, the Kilt Kids.

NIGEL: It was, again, not a great group. They thought, "Oh, we'll dress this way and people will think—"

DAVID: Kilts and tam-o'-shanters. It was what you call in this country a hokey sort of thing.

MARTY: Well, I've seen you, Nigel, dress in kilts.

NIGEL: But that's a real thing. In my family, on my mum's side, she was Scottish. She was a Campbell. That's a real thing. The Kilt Kids were rubbish.

DAVID: They had a mini-opera called *Clytemnestra*. And it had all these vaguely classical references, Greek and Roman.

NIGEL: They had a Greek chorus of sirens.

DAVID: Oh, my God. It was awful.

NIGEL: It was horrible. But Ross was . . .

DEREK: He was a star.

DAVID: A big star.

MARTY: And Peter "James" Bond, how did you find him?

DAVID: He was mostly doing sessions. Yeah, he was a session man.

**NIGEL:** Occasionally we would do sessions. Not regularly, but I remember I did this thing for some sort of shampoo or dish soap. I was playing guitar and he was there. I thought, "Oh, yeah, he can play."

**MARTY:** I didn't know you guys played on commercials.

**DAVID:** I never did. Nigel did.

**MARTY:** And that's where you met Peter "James" Bond.

**DAVID:** Peter helped us finish that album. Very heady stuff. And of course, the title track, "The Sun Never Sweats," is Derek's work. A really wonderful piece, but it's a bit demanding.

**DEREK:** Very demanding.

**NIGEL:** It's very intensive. And Derek came into his own then, really. He blossomed.

**MARTY:** What was the inspiration behind "The Sun Never Sweats"?

**DEREK:** "The sun never sets."

**MARTY:** The sun never sets?

**DEREK:** Exactly. That was the inspiration. I said, "Let's put a *w* in it."

**MARTY:** I see, "sets" became "sweats." It wasn't, like, because the sun—

**DEREK:** Sweats? No, the sun doesn't sweat.

**MARTY:** Right. It *causes* sweat.

**DAVID:** But it's also a reference to the British Empire. "Mad Dogs and Englishmen."

**DEREK:** It's about the death of English power in the world.

**DAVID:** Yet it has a very exciting sea-shanty quality to it. It's sort of like, "Yeah, this is all crap and it's all over, thank God. And yet, isn't it fun to play pirates?"

**NIGEL:** It works on multiple levels.

**MARTY:** What was the follow-up to *The Sun Never Sweats*?

**DAVID:** We did another live album called *Jap Habit*. It was actually three LPs and a shirt and a belt buckle, and . . .

**DEREK:** And a 45.

**NIGEL:** And a hat, that had that little chin thing. You could fold it and it went right on.

**MARTY:** Why was the album called *Jap Habit*?

**DAVID:** We were inspired by our first time in the Far East. We recorded it live.

**MARTY:** I don't think you could use that title now.

**DEREK:** We'd get canceled.

**DAVID:** But the Japanese company that released it, they loved it. They put a fortune into all the gimmickry.

**MARTY:** And how did that album do?

**DAVID:** Terribly.

**DEREK:** It was too expensive.

**NIGEL:** The Japanese people didn't hold it against us.

**DAVID:** But Ross was very disappointed. He left the band.

**DEREK:** He left the music business!

**DAVID:** He went to Namibia to become a missionary.

**MARTY:** Really? I didn't know that.

**DAVID:** Yeah. After he converted what he felt was the requisite number of Africans, he put together an album that he self-recorded.

**MARTY:** What was it called?

**NIGEL:** *Doesn't Anybody Here Speak English?*

**DAVID:** Which did not sell, but it was true to his heart.

**DEREK:** Well, it was a cri de coeur.

**MARTY:** A what?

**DEREK:** You heard me. A cri de coeur. A cri of the coeur.

**MARTY:** Right, I guess. He was frustrated because nobody there spoke English.

**DEREK:** Well, they did, it turns out.

**MARTY:** They did?

**NIGEL:** They all did. Yeah, he was deluded. It was his excuse for—

**MARTY:** For failure?

**NIGEL:** Exactly.

**DEREK:** He actually got bad reviews in English.

**MARTY:** So is that when Viv Savage became your keyboard player?

**DAVID:** Yeah. He was with a group called Aftertaste.

**NIGEL:** Terrible group. It's funny in thinking now about this, that a lot of the people we found—

DEREK: We rescued.

NIGEL: —were in these rubbish groups, but they were good.

DAVID: Their vocalist, though. The Aftertaste vocalist was Lane something. Something with a *C*. Lane Cartwright?

DEREK: Lane Changing.

DAVID: Right. He could really bring it. He was a really good singer. He had a couple of speech impediments, but a great instrument, as they say.

NIGEL: Yeah, but he couldn't say *w*'s.

DAVID: Yeah, he had a lot of trouble with their version of "What a Wonderful World."

DEREK: He tried to rewrite it.

DAVID: But Aftertaste, they were crap except for Lane. And, of course, Viv, who came over to our side. And he was fine. What he could do, he could play a really strong bass part with his left hand.

NIGEL: He wasn't as dexterous as some of the other people, but he was solid.

DEREK: And he loved to rock 'n' roll.

DAVID: And he looked like a fucking lunatic.

DEREK: Which was a plus.

MARTY: And he joined the band when you recorded *Bent for the Rent*?

DEREK: Not a great title for a record.

DAVID: Not great for sales, either.

# THE WORLD'S LOUDEST BAND

**MARTY:** What does that mean, "bent for the rent"?

**DAVID:** If the landlord's bugging you and you can't pay them, maybe you'll do them a favor.

**MARTY:** I see.

**DAVID:** It's an expression we used to hear around London. You don't hear it much anymore.

**MARTY:** So the album wasn't successful?

**DAVID:** No.

**DEREK:** It stayed well off the charts.

**MARTY:** And your label at the time was Megaphone?

**DAVID:** We were with Megaphone for four or five albums.

**MARTY:** And you sued them over royalties?

**DAVID:** We sued them because we thought royalties were being withheld.

**DEREK:** And they sued us back.

**MARTY:** For what?

**DEREK:** They alleged "lack of talent."

**MARTY:** They sued you for lack of talent?

**NIGEL:** It was quite insulting, really. It said that on the piece of paper.

**MARTY:** In the lawsuit?

**NIGEL:** Yeah.

**DAVID:** And we couldn't prove otherwise, because you can't prove a negative.

**MARTY:** Did you reach a settlement?

**DAVID:** Yeah, we agreed to not speak to each other, and we actually had to put it in writing that we would no longer make any product for Megaphone. They were very happy with that.

**MARTY:** There's a quote I saw from the lawyer for Megaphone that says, "Stay the fuck out of the studio."

**DAVID:** Yeah, well, that's lawyer-speak.

**MARTY:** So you don't think he really meant that?

**NIGEL:** Oh, he meant it.

L*ike Spinal Tap*, my filmmaking career was marked by a mix of highs and lows. In the mid-seventies, one of the local TV spots I did was seen by Dick McGoy, an account executive at a major advertising agency. He asked if I wanted to shoot a series of commercials for Purina's Chuck Wagon dog food. They had this concept of a hungry dog chasing after a miniature checkerboard-patterned covered wagon filled with kibble. I had finally arrived. I could see my feature film career poking up over the horizon. At this point I changed my name to Marty DiBergi as an homage to the great directors I admired: Martin Scorsese, Vittorio De Sica, Ingmar Bergman, and Federico Fellini.

I was on a high. But soon it all came crashing down when the ad company ran out of places for the dog to chase the chuck wagon. The series was discontinued—and with it, my dreams of directing a feature film. I had become typed as the dog-food guy. I was distraught. I had to find a new way in.

# CHAPTER 5

# The Wilderness Years

The late 1970s was a period of soul-searching for David, Nigel, and Derek, a time for solo projects and early experiments in cave-aging cheese. But Spinal Tap's head-banging days were far from over.

**MARTY:** Nigel, was there a period where you lived in a castle?

**NIGEL:** It was a rental in Lichtenstein.

**DEREK:** Option to buy, right?

**NIGEL:** Yeah, but not my option. I saw this picture of this castle, so I thought: "Why not Lichtenstein?" And I went there. It's a tiny country. You can drive across it in a half a day. Or half an hour, really.

**MARTY:** And at that time, you weren't playing as a band.

**NIGEL:** Not officially.

DAVID: We'd drop in. Occasionally we'd go out and see him.

DEREK: We'd jam with him a bit.

DAVID: We actually started playing around with a concept album inspired by Derek.

MARTY: Really, what was it called?

DEREK: It was called *It's a Smalls World*.

MARTY: Taken from the Disney ride It's a Small World?

DEREK: No, taken from my name. There was nothing Disney about it.

DAVID: You wouldn't want to play that record for children.

NIGEL: I wish I had those tapes.

DAVID: You kept saying, "Let's put this down." And then we'd have lunch and we'd forget.

DEREK: The recording machine was hard to work.

NIGEL: Terribly hard.

DEREK: We never figured it out.

DAVID: You had to have the right change, for one thing.

MARTY: What you are you saying? It was a coin-operated tape machine?

DAVID: Coin-operated, yeah.

MARTY: Nigel, I noticed that when I visited you there, you had some emus.

NIGEL: Yeah. They were there when I got there.

MARTY: Oh, so, they weren't yours.

NIGEL: I didn't personally purchase them. They're lovely creatures, though. A lot of people think, "Oh, they're going to kill me." But emus, they're quite nice.

MARTY: You seemed to be very proud of them.

DAVID: That's called Emu Pride. It's very specific. Some people would be house-proud. He was emu-proud.

NIGEL: People think they would bite you, but they don't bite at all. If they didn't like you, they would kick you.

MARTY: Really? So they're birds that, like ostriches, can't fly.

DAVID: Yeah. A rhea is, too.

MARTY: A rhea is a bird?

DAVID: Yeah.

MARTY: How do you spell that?

DAVID: Like the actress Rhea Perlman.

MARTY: I don't think Rhea Perlman can fly.

DAVID: Never said she could.

MARTY: So after the hiatus in Lichtenstein, you started back up with a new drummer.

DAVID: Peter "James" Bond.

MARTY: And it's been well-documented about what happened to him.

DEREK: Yeah, he exploded.

NIGEL: Onstage.

DAVID: At the Isle of Lucy Jazz-Blues Festival.

**NIGEL:** Only a little green globule left on his drum seat.

**DAVID:** Spontaneous human combustion.

**DEREK:** Which happens much more than you think.

**MARTY:** Well, it happens a *lot* more than I think. Because I don't think it ever happens.

**NIGEL:** People don't want to think about it because it's an awful way to go.

**MARTY:** Can you name other people who have spontaneously combusted?

**DEREK:** Marie Antoinette.

**MARTY:** Marie Antoinette was guillotined.

**DEREK:** Right. But, she exploded first and *then* she was guillotined.

**MARTY:** Oh.

**DEREK:** They don't say that part now.

**DAVID:** You're saying they quashed it.

**DEREK:** Oh, yeah. Covered it right up.

**MARTY:** So you're saying that they guillotined an already-exploded person.

**DEREK:** Makes it much easier, doesn't it?

**MARTY:** I guess.

**NIGEL:** If you go and look at Egyptian art, which you see in pyramids, it shows the people, they're all looking in the same direction—

**DAVID:** They're walking like Egyptians.

**NIGEL:** —they're looking right or left. And then there's just this... *thing*. And that's what that is: an explosion of one of those Egyptian people.

**MARTY:** Couldn't quite follow that, but—

**NIGEL:** That's your problem.

**DAVID:** Did you know that Christopher Lee once went to Paris to watch one of the last uses of the guillotine?

**MARTY:** That's another thing I was not aware of.

**DAVID:** Someone said to him, "Would you like to come and see a beheading?" And he said, "Who wouldn't?"

**NIGEL:** And when he was asked if he wanted to go to a concert called "The Last of the Castrati," he said, "Who wouldn't?"

**DAVID:** I think he was more interested to see the prep.

**DEREK:** The auditions, as it were.

**NIGEL:** They used a lot of mineral oil and—

**MARTY:** You mean, to turn someone into a castrato?

**NIGEL:** Which eventually they stopped doing. But they have some recordings of the last of those people. It's a very eerie voice.

**DAVID:** Can you imagine putting that through Auto-Tune? You'd really hear a whole different story.

**MARTY:** These people literally are always singing in falsetto.

**DEREK:** Yeah, like Frankie Valli.

**MARTY:** Frankie Valli is not a castrato.

**DEREK:** As far as we know.

**DAVID:** He *was* on *The Sopranos*.

**MARTY:** Changing the subject—let's talk about "Nice 'n' Stinky." It came out in the spring of '77 and was . . .

**DAVID:** A surprise hit, yeah. It was one of those unconstructed things. People heard it on the radio and they said, "There's something missing here." Well, what was missing was pretty much everything except the beat and the feel.

**DEREK:** We thought people's reaction would be "Where's the content?" But they loved the lack of content.

**DAVID:** Yeah, we made a choice. In fact, I think if we removed the content out of a lot of our product, we probably would have sold a lot more.

**MARTY:** Really?

**DAVID:** Yeah, take it right out. The Spice Girls did it.

**MARTY:** Interesting.

**DEREK:** No content, just . . . girls.

**MARTY:** Yet this becomes a hit, and now all of a sudden you're back together again. But you need another drummer.

**DAVID:** Yeah. And where did we find him? The Eurovision Song Contest, of all places. The house-band drummer was this bloke, all skin and bones. Six one, dripping wet.

**MARTY:** Again, you understand that "dripping wet" doesn't refer to height?

**DEREK:** You get his point.

**MARTY:** That he was thin.

**NIGEL:** Yeah, but you could still see him bangin' away.

**DAVID:** Playing every kind of style.

**NIGEL:** Anything. He could play anything.

**DEREK:** For hours!

**MARTY:** And this is Mick Shrimpton.

**DAVID:** Mick Shrimpton, yeah. Michael Shrimpton. He had a funny middle name, like Arbuthnot.

**NIGEL:** It's a Welsh name.

**MARTY:** So the first record with him was *Shark Sandwich*.

**DAVID:** Yeah. He really made that work.

**MARTY:** But it didn't get a great review.

**DAVID:** It got a lot of bad reviews. Still, it's a very strong album.

**MARTY:** One of them just said, "Shit sandwich."

**DEREK:** Let me say this: nobody's reading that review today, and nobody's listening to that record.

**DAVID:** Perfectly said.

**MARTY:** This was your first album for Parallel Records.

**DAVID:** Our only album for Parallel. After *Shark Sandwich* didn't move, they wanted us to change our name.

**MARTY:** To what?

**DAVID:** They suggested Popcorn Blizzard.

DEREK: That was one.

DAVID: Underwater Airline.

DEREK: That was another.

NIGEL: We suggested they change *their* name.

DAVID: That didn't go well.

DEREK: They just went out of business.

NIGEL: We went to their office in Soho and they had padlocked the door.

MARTY: Then you signed with Polymer to record *Smell the Glove*.

And this is where I climb aboard Spinal Tap's train. Destination: the rock 'n' roll pantheon.

## CHAPTER 6

# Faith, Fame, and Festivals

David, Nigel, and Derek were reluctant to talk about their manager, Ian Faith. *As devotees of my film are well aware, it was Ian who engineered Tap's return to America for the first time in almost six years, to promote their controversial album* Smell the Glove.

When I learned of Tap's pending tour, I thought, This is my chance to return to my documentary roots and free myself from movie purgatory. *I convinced a friend, Mark Spiggler, to pretend to be my agent and call Ian to offer my services. Ian then took my offer to the band.*

*I was thrilled when the band agreed. Although the pay wasn't great—there wasn't any—I was certain this would be a marriage made in heaven: a band that I loved and a filmmaking format I cherished. Unfortunately, the marriage met with some nearly irreconcilable differences.*

MARTY: Let's talk about Ian Faith.

DAVID: Do we have to?

MARTY: How did he come into your lives?

DEREK: By an evil wind.

DAVID: It was one of those things where we would notice him after a gig. He was always ligging about, you know? We were like, "Who's that bloke?" "I don't know. He was here the other night." And then one night, he comes up to us and says, "You guys are going nowhere, and the reason I know this is because I'm here every night watching you go nowhere."

DEREK: "And I live in nowhere."

DAVID: Well, he didn't say that.

DEREK: No, he didn't say that.

DAVID: He could have.

DEREK: He should have.

DAVID: He convinced us that if we put ourselves in his hands, we would make a go of it, 'cause at the time, we were only occasionally gigging, not recording at all.

DEREK: We were handling ourselves.

DAVID: Sometimes in public.

DAVID: Then he said the two words that are a red flag for you not to trust a person.

MARTY: Which are?

DEREK: "Trust me."

NIGEL: The thing about managers is, it's almost like they're on you before you even know they're there. It's sort of like as if someone farted. You don't see them, you just sense their presence. And then they're there.

MARTY: So what you're saying is, you could smell Ian before you saw him?

NIGEL: Yeah, it's this sense that "Mmm, something's off here."

DAVID: They prey on your self-doubts. If you're thinking, "Maybe there's some reason I'm not making it," the manager senses that and tells you the only reason you're not making it is that you don't have him.

NIGEL: Exactly.

DAVID: And if it happens at exactly the right moment, you're done.

MARTY: And Ian sensed that moment.

DAVID: He did.

DEREK: And he *dealt it*.

DAVID: Silent but deadly.

MARTY: Like your album's title?

DAVID: The phrase has many uses.

DEREK: He kept saying to us, "You have no trajectory. You have no trajectory."

DAVID: Four-syllable word. Very powerful.

DEREK: I didn't know what a trajectory was.

MARTY: Sounds like he played on your vulnerability.

DAVID: Yeah. *He* seemed to be doing really well. We saw him shake down a couple of promoters and it was pretty impressive.

DEREK: Sometimes blood was involved.

DAVID: It's not a nice business.

NIGEL: And he was not a nice man.

DEREK: So we thought he was a good fit.

NIGEL: It's a low calling, really.

DAVID: Sort of like a basso yodeler: a low calling.

MARTY: I see what you're saying. So we're at the point where I come into the picture. You were planning a tour of the United States with the *Smell the Glove* album.

DAVID: And you had seen us in New York.

MARTY: At the Electric Banana.

NIGEL: It was a fun place.

MARTY: And you guys blew me away. Of course, I had been a fan long before *Smell the Glove*, so I was so excited to document the tour. But when the film was finished, I was upset by your reaction.

NIGEL: I remember feeling hurt and feeling betrayed.

MARTY: You felt that I portrayed you in a bad light.

DAVID: You seemed to only focus on the negative stuff, the mishaps.

DEREK: There were dozens of gigs where we found the stage straightaway. We didn't see that reflected.

**NIGEL:** It was twisted. You could document any group and they have things go wrong—drummers falling off their stools, singers falling off the stage. But they're not shown. If they're not shown, no one knows. And some people were laughing at us.

**MARTY:** You think I should have shown the times where you successfully found the stage?

**DEREK:** Why not?

**DAVID:** Jeanine wasn't so crazy about the way she was portrayed. That made for a rough decade for me.

**MARTY:** But the film created a rebirth for Tap. You had success in Japan. And later, you came back to the U.S. and did pretty well.

**DAVID:** Yeah, we started gigging again. We wound up recording another album called *Break Like the Wind*, which came out in '92.

**MARTY:** Right.

**DAVID:** And we had a lovely tour. We played the Royal Albert Hall in London. We played Wembley Stadium and Glastonbury.

**MARTY:** Sounds exciting.

**DAVID:** It was.

**MARTY:** But there were stretches when you didn't perform.

**DAVID:** True.

**MARTY:** What were you all doing during those hiatuses?

**DAVID:** I traveled quite a bit with Jeanine, until the money ran out. I studied black magic for a bit in Bavaria. It was only about a week and a half.

**MARTY:** How much black magic can you learn in a week and a half?

**DAVID:** About a week and a half's worth.

**MARTY:** I remember the Live Earth concert.

**DAVID:** '07, yeah.

**MARTY:** At that time, you were working at a high-colonic clinic.

**DAVID:** True. But I was also managing some rap acts. I had one that was fairly successful, big fat Black guy.

**MARTY:** What was his name?

**DAVID:** Big Fat Black Guy.

**MARTY:** Oh, that was his actual—

**DAVID:** Yeah, and I had a lovely group called Adequit, A-D-E-Q-U-I-T.

**MARTY:** That seems like a name that would limit their upside.

**DAVID:** I know. But it came across as modesty. Which is very important in the hip-hop community.

**DEREK:** They were good enough.

**MARTY:** And Nigel, when I caught up with you, you were working on a farm that raised miniature horses.

**NIGEL:** Yes. I became, I suppose, obsessed with miniature horses. They're very sweet and easier to take care of than big horses. You need a smaller area.

**DAVID:** Smaller paddock.

**NIGEL:** Yeah. Paddock and stalls and whatever. But I wanted to race them, and I found it difficult to find the little people to race them. The people had to be 2.5 feet high or shorter.

**MARTY:** And, Derek, when I reconnected with you, you were in rehab.

**DEREK:** Yes, I was in rehab for internet addiction. I was addicted to the internet.

**NIGEL:** I remember when I heard about this. I wrote him an email. But he didn't answer.

**DEREK:** I wasn't allowed. It's terrible. It gets ahold of you, and before you know it, you're looking at cats waterskiing.

**MARTY:** That's serious.

**DEREK:** It was. I had to go to rehab twice. That's how bad it was. I thought I was cured, went back home, and—

**DAVID:** The addiction rebooted on him.

**MARTY:** I thought it kind of ironic that when I talked to you, we were talking to each other through the computer.

**DEREK:** Yeah. I was violating my regimen.

**MARTY:** You also went through a period where you kind of took up where your father left off with SaniFone?

**DEREK:** Yeah. But, by that time, people had for the most part stopped using landlines. Suddenly there was no money in phone-sanitizing.

**DAVID:** My dad used to say, "Don't pick your nose. There's no money in it."

**MARTY:** How does that apply?

**DAVID:** Who said it did?

*In 2009, after playing to huge crowds at the Glastonbury Festival and Wembley Arena, Tap abruptly stopped performing. At the time, no one knew why.*

## CHAPTER 7

# Rockin' in the Urn

I too had disappeared from public view. As I said, I was at the spiritual retreat of Baba Ram Das Boot, looking for meaning, when I learned of Tap's plans to reunite for one final concert in New Orleans in 2024.

When I got the go-ahead to document the concert and work with Tap once again, I was ecstatic. I jumped for joy and sang "Happy Days Are Here Again"—not the slow Barbra Streisand version, but the original up-tempo version by Lou Levin with Leo Reisman and His Orchestra.

The story of how and why the members of Tap became estranged is explained in my new film, Spinal Tap II: The End Continues. Not wanting to be a spoiler-alert guy, I'll disclose that they are playing together again, if only for this one last time. With age, the guys, approaching what some might call wisdom, have grown reflective about the life-affirming powers of heavy rock.

**MARTY:** We're seeing rockers who started when they were very young—Mick Jagger, Paul McCartney, Elton John, people well into their seventies and eighties—still performing onstage. And it seems like you guys still enjoy playing, too. What motivates you?

**DEREK:** Rock 'n' roll came out of country music and blues. And those people played 'til they dropped. We're just inheriting that tradition. You play 'til you bloody drop.

**DAVID:** This might get a bit metaphysical, but rock is built around a beat. Like your heart is built around a beat. When you are young, when you're falling in love for the first time, you're dancing close, you're making out and all this stuff, you're aware of two things: the music and your heartbeat. Well, there's other stuff. But—

**DEREK:** Three things.

**DAVID:** Yeah, well, but the point I'm making is, as long as the heart is beating, the rock is there for you. I used to say, "Rock 'n' roll keeps you young, but you have to die young." Now I think, "If you're old, keep rockin' 'til you get older. And then keep rockin' after that."

**NIGEL:** I think you have to do it. Anyone who's done it early on has to keep doing it if they can. Assuming your hands and voice work, you've got to do it because it's in your heart. Why would you stop if it gives you joy, you know? To play in front of people? People seem to like it. I've been playing in the pub up in the North of England and that's as much fun as anything else.

**MARTY:** Right. And, Derek, I noticed that you wrote this new song "Rockin' in the Urn," which indicates that even after you die, you still keep rocking.

**DEREK:** Even death can't stop a rocker from rockin'.

**DAVID:** Or droppin' *g*'s and addin' apostrophes.

**NIGEL:** It might slow you down a bit, death.

**DEREK:** And dampen the tempo.

**DAVID:** But if there's music in your soul, when you die the music would have to go somewhere, wouldn't it?

**NIGEL:** That's just logic, isn't it?

**DEREK:** That's why when I'm ashes, I'll still be bashing.

**DAVID:** Right. Nothing changes.

**DEREK:** Just the venue and the makeup of the crowd.

**NIGEL:** Yeah, and the merch.

**MARTY:** I want to thank you all for taking the time to talk with me.

**DAVID:** Sometimes a pleasure, Marty.

# Acknowledgments

## Marty DiBergi

Where to begin? First, I want to thank my three musical heroes: David St. Hubbins, Nigel Tufnel, and Derek Smalls. Without the trust and support of these luminescent rock gods, this humble purveyor of movie magic would be slicing mortadella at his father's deli. So thank you, gents, for the gift you have given to me and your legions of fans.

To the entire crew of both *Tap* films: Your dedication to helping me capture Spinal Tap's talent and humanity—at minimum wage, no less—has made my filmmaking experience an absolute joy.

To my parents, thank you for believing that a boy with no obvious disadvantages could almost make a living doing what others have been much more successful at.

Finally, I would be remiss if I didn't pay tribute to all the Spinal Tap drummers who have met with untimely endings. To John "Stumpy" Pepys (bizarre gardening accident); Eric "Stumpy Joe" Childs (choked on vomit—someone else's); Peter "James" Bond (spontaneously combusted onstage); Mick Shrimpton (ditto); Joe "Mama" Besser (cause unknown); Richard "Ric" Shrimpton (sold his dialysis machine for drugs; presumed dead); and Scott "Skippy" Skuffleton (prolonged sneezing fit)—may you all rest in peace. And to Tap's most recent drummer, Didi Crockett—all I can say is you knew what you were getting into.

## David St. Hubbins

To the women in my life . . . Mum, of course, but also:

Lhasa, Cleo, Diane K., Diane M., Paulette, Lynda, Gayle, Gayle Jr., Liz, Popsy, the girl at the clinic, Hedda, Edie, Deb (fake heiress), Deb (fake deb), Xuxi, Lala, Kelly from Interpol, Muireann (pronounced "Maryann"), Julia (pronounced "Hulia"), Kristen, Kristin, Kirsten, Chicago Red, Caoimhe (pronounced "Kweevah"), the Capricorn waitress, Beige Betty, Ramona, Winter Green, Ynes, Skye . . . and Jeanine.

## Nigel Tufnel

First, without Enid and Ollie, my mum and dad, I wouldn't be here. At least that's what my granddad Bertie told me. I think often about how lovely they were.

It was my good fortune to find music. Thanks to all my heroes, especially Blind Bubba Cheeks. His genius was my inspiration.

I must thank my dear Moira for being by my side through the good and bad times.

Finally, to my oldest friend, David, you are, and always will be, in my heart.

## Derek Smalls

I would be remissful to not acknowledge my parents, Duffman "Duff" Smalls and Rosa Springer Smalls. He was a wonderful example of how sanitizing people's telephones could be not only a job but also a calling. And she, during the four years I knew her before she decamped to join the Hotten Totties, kindled the flame of music that has never since been extinguished. Or, if it has, I haven't noticed.

My huge thanks to David and Nigel for rescuing me from Britain's only all-white ska band, Skaface. It was a bad idea gone wrong. Dave and Nige, I mean it from my heart's bottom when I say that, despite our differences, we will always have our differences.

My thanks to the lads in the Christian rock band Lambsblood for briefly accepting me into their ranks, despite my reputation for devil worship.

And finally, thanks to the fans, especially those who, every night, gathered backstage for some post-show big-bottomology.

# A FINE LINE BETWEEN STUPID AND CLEVER

# A FINE LINE BETWEEN STUPID AND CLEVER

## The Story of

**ROB REINER**
**CHRISTOPHER GUEST**
**MICHAEL McKEAN**
and **HARRY SHEARER**

with **DAVID KAMP**

New York   Amsterdam/Antwerp   London
Toronto   Sydney/Melbourne   New Delhi

Gallery Books
An Imprint of Simon & Schuster, LLC
1230 Avenue of the Americas
New York, NY 10020

For more than 100 years, Simon & Schuster has championed authors and the stories they create. By respecting the copyright of an author's intellectual property, you enable Simon & Schuster and the author to continue publishing exceptional books for years to come. We thank you for supporting the author's copyright by purchasing an authorized edition of this book.

No amount of this book may be reproduced or stored in any format, nor may it be uploaded to any website, database, language-learning model, or other repository, retrieval, or artificial intelligence system without express permission. All rights reserved. Inquiries may be directed to Simon & Schuster, 1230 Avenue of the Americas, New York, NY 10020 or permissions@simonandschuster.com.

Copyright © 2025 by Authorized Spinal Tap, LLC

All rights reserved, including the right to reproduce this book or portions thereof in any form whatsoever. For information, address Gallery Books Subsidiary Rights Department, 1230 Avenue of the Americas, New York, NY 10020.

First Gallery Books hardcover edition September 2025

GALLERY BOOKS and colophon are registered trademarks of Simon & Schuster, LLC

Simon & Schuster strongly believes in freedom of expression and stands against censorship in all its forms. For more information, visit BooksBelong.com.

For information about special discounts for bulk purchases, please contact Simon & Schuster Special Sales at 1-866-506-1949 or business@simonandschuster.com.

The Simon & Schuster Speakers Bureau can bring authors to your live event. For more information or to book an event, contact the Simon & Schuster Speakers Bureau at 1-866-248-3049 or visit our website at www.simonspeakers.com.

Interior design by Jaime Putorti

Manufactured in the United States of America

10  9  8  7  6  5  4  3  2  1

Library of Congress Cataloging-in-Publication Data is available.

ISBN 978-1-6680-7914-0
ISBN 978-1-6680-7916-4 (ebook)

# Contents

Introduction — 1
**CHAPTER 1:** In Ancient Times . . . — 3
**CHAPTER 2:** It's Getting Louder Every Day — 15
**CHAPTER 3:** 'Twas the Rock 'n' Roll Creation — 27
**CHAPTER 4:** Trying to Raise Some Hard Love — 35
**CHAPTER 5:** Pound Notes, Loose Change, Bad Checks, Anything — 41
**CHAPTER 6:** Just Want to Make Some Eardrums Bleed — 57
**CHAPTER 7:** Tonight I'm Gonna Rock You — 85
**CHAPTER 8:** And I Looked and I Saw That It Was Good — 101
**CHAPTER 9:** How Can I Leave This Behind? — 113
**CHAPTER 10:** It's Not Too Late — 123
**CHAPTER 11:** Yes, Please, Sir, and Thank You, Ma'am — 129
**CHAPTER 12:** I Rode the Jet Stream, I Hit the Top — 141
**CHAPTER 13:** 'Twas the Ultimate Mutation — 151
**CHAPTER 14:** All the Way Home — 163
**INTERLUDE:** I Look to the Stars and the Answer Is Clear — 171
**CHAPTER 15:** We'll Go Back in Time to That Mystic Land — 181
**CHAPTER 16:** The Looser the Waistband — 191
*Acknowledgments* — 195

# A FINE LINE BETWEEN STUPID AND CLEVER

# Introduction

In 1982, I began shooting a film under the auspices of an independent studio called Embassy Pictures. Don't look for it; it doesn't exist anymore. But what does exist is my first film as a director, *This Is Spinal Tap*. It transformed my life and the lives of my three friends, cowriters, and costars, Christopher Guest, Michael McKean, and Harry Shearer.

Over the years, *This Is Spinal Tap* has established itself as a significant part of our culture: first as a cult hit and then as a widely watched and rewatched classic. It pioneered a new narrative format, the mockumentary, and proved as quotable as *The Godfather* and arguably funnier: "These go to eleven"; "None more black"; "Hello, Cleveland!"; "Enough of my yakkin'"; and my favorite, "It's such a fine line between stupid and clever."

*This Is Spinal Tap* transformed the way people talk and think about the music industry. Large venues are described as Enormo-Domes. "Stonehenge" has become synonymous with epic stagecraft failure. Time and time again, professional musicians have approached us to recount their embarrassing "Spinal Tap moments."

People have often asked us if we would ever consider doing a sequel. For a long time, we resisted. We had already made a movie on our own terms that has become part of cinematic and musical history. Leave well enough alone! Or, as Jack Benny famously said, "If there's one thing that doesn't have to go on, it's the show."

Then, a few years ago, after a long legal battle, we finally got the rights back to the original film. So Chris, Michael, Harry, and I decided to get together to see if there was any gas left in the tank. After rejecting most of the ideas we came up with, something clicked, and a story began to emerge that we felt we could go with. So, on March 6, 2024, my seventy-seventh birthday, in the city of New Orleans, we started shooting the sequel to *This Is Spinal Tap*, which at the time was tentatively titled *Goodbye, Cleveland*. It is now called *Spinal Tap II: The End Continues*, with the "II" in the form of a little model of Stonehenge.

We also decided that it was time to tell the full story of the making of *This Is Spinal Tap* and its long and wholly unanticipated afterlife. What you are about to read is that story.

It's been quite a ride. None of us could have imagined, when our movie came out in limited release on March 2, 1984, that someday, Chris, Michael, and Harry would play to a sellout audience at the Royal Albert Hall, to 80,000 fans at Wembley Stadium, and to over 100,000 at the Glastonbury Festival. Never in my wildest dreams would I have thought that my first film would be selected by the Library of Congress for inclusion in the National Film Registry.

But hey, enough of my braggin'. Whaddya say? Let's memoir!

—Rob Reiner, Los Angeles, 2025

CHAPTER 1

# In Ancient Times . . .

The first sighting of Spinal Tap in the wild came in the summer of 1979, as part of an ABC comedy special called *The TV Show*. It was a satirical look at all things television. The premise was that you, the viewer, watched along with a guy seen only from behind (me, actually) as he sat in a comfy chair and casually flipped from channel to channel with his remote.

The show included a telethon devoted to stopping death, "the ultimate disease"; a *Mister Rogers* parody; a promo for an exploitation movie called *3 Girls in Orbit*; a cloyingly earnest evangelist; and a totally un-PC sitcom called *Queen Elizabeth and Andy*, in which the Queen of England is married to the Kingfish from *Amos 'n' Andy*.

There was also a takeoff of *The Midnight Special*, a late-night NBC music show that featured the big rock acts of the day. In our parody, the show was emceed by the radio deejay Wolfman Jack (me again, in a pompadour and a beard), who introduced the next act in his inimitable growling, howling wolfman way.

"Are ya ready to rock and rawlll? Now, from England, have moycy, you're gonna love 'em to death! Spinal Taaaap! *Awooooooo!*"

And for the first time, appearing as Spinal Tap, were Christopher Guest, Michael McKean, and Harry Shearer in wigs and rock makeup, performing in a music video for a song called "Rock 'n' Roll Nightmare," which featured lyrics such as "When the rock 'n' roll nightmare comes / The devil's gonna make me eat my drums."

Me and my writing partner, Phil Mishkin, had come up with the idea for *The TV Show*. To help with the script, we brought in Harry, Chris, Martin Mull, Billy Crystal, and a writing partner of Chris's, Tom Leopold. To help with the Spinal Tap sequence, Chris enlisted Michael, with whom he'd been writing and playing music since their college days.

When Spinal Tap first appeared, the band members didn't have names yet. Harry, a fine bass player, didn't even play on the actual track—Chris and Michael, who wrote the song, recorded it in a studio with Leland Sklar, the brilliant L.A. session bassist renowned for backing up such greats as Carole King, James Taylor, Jackson Browne, and Linda Ronstadt.

The legendary rock drummer Russ Kunkel was also recruited for the video, along with the singer-songwriter Loudon Wainwright III, who mimed playing the keyboards. Both Russ and Loudon wore Afro wigs. I can't remember why, but I can't say it made them more attractive.

The late seventies was a time when rock 'n' roll was rife with pretension. Punk had hit the scene, but the over-the-top dinosaur acts were still very much out there, setting off pyrotechnics, flying inflatable pigs over the audience, and wearing tight spandex outfits that highlighted what could only be described, as Nigel Tufnel might say, as armadillos in their trousers.

There was a fantasy sequence in the "Rock 'n' Roll Nightmare" video. It was every bit as incoherent as the ones in Led Zeppelin's concert film *The Song Remains the Same*, in which Robert Plant is depicted storming a castle atop a gallant steed and Jimmy Page dramatically scales a mountain, only to encounter a hooded version of himself as an old man. Spinal Tap's excursion into fantasy was a bit more mundane. As the band is playing cards, their game is disrupted by a sledgehammer-wielding policeman in a pig's mask. Then, as logic would dictate, we cut to a courtroom, where a judge in a skull mask pounds his gavel and declares, "This court finds you guilty." Then he asks the band: "How do you plead?" In unison, the band members look up at the judge and plaintively say, "Not guilty?"

The finale was an overhead shot of the band laid out on the floor, performing snow-angel motions in a lame attempt at Busby Berkeley–type choreography. To achieve an eerie effect that would suggest that the guys were condemned to an infernal hellscape, we used a piece of equipment known as a bee smoker to flood the stage with smoke.

It turned out to be an actual hellscape. As the guys lay flat on their backs, the bee smoker started spraying hot oil on them. While the crew scrambled to address this problem, Michael, Chris, and Harry, professionals that they were, remained in position.

As Harry explains, "Rather than kill the propman, we stayed in character." Adds Michael, "While we were waiting for them to set up again, which was taking forever, we kept joking."

And then, according to Chris, "We started schnadling in British accents. *Schnadling* is a term I use that means 'improvise.' When I'm putting together one of my films, it's critical that each cast member be able to schnadle. In that moment under the dripping hot oil, schnadling away, we realized, 'It's fun to be these guys. We should find something else to do with them.'"

But we're getting ahead of the story.

Of the four of us, Michael and Chris have known each other the longest. They met in 1967. They were both transfer students to what is now called the Tisch School of the Arts at New York University. Michael had spent his freshman year at a Pittsburgh college then known as the Carnegie Institute of Technology, or Carnegie Tech; as Michael likes to say, "I went to NYU before the Tisch money and to Carnegie Mellon before the Mellon money." Chris had spent a year at Bard College in upstate New York, where, at the campus club, his bluegrass group was billed below a jazz-rock combo headed by two seniors named Donald Fagen and Walter Becker. Yes, the Steely Dan guys.

At NYU, Michael and Chris connected right away. They had the same model of electric guitar, the Gibson ES-335. And their senses of humor were in sync. Michael recalls, "Our first conversation was about music. Chris had just seen Mike Bloomfield, who was playing with the Electric Flag at the Bitter End. He took out his guitar and did an impression of how Bloomfield played, holding these big notes and making these contorted faces."

When Michael's girlfriend got cast in a production at the Guthrie Theater in Minneapolis, he was presented with a choice: (A) find a new place to live or (B) cohabitate with his girlfriend's dad, who had moved into their apartment. Michael chose option A and wound up moving in with Chris, who lived near the White Horse Tavern on the corner of Hudson and West 11th Streets. It was a loft-bed situation:

Chris in the upper bunk and Michael the lower. This was back when Greenwich Village was still bohemian and affordable.

The first McKean-Guest compositions were satire-free and a bit more chaste than future Spinal Tap compositions such as "Big Bottom" and "Sex Farm." Jimi Hendrix's *Are You Experienced* and the Beatles' *Sgt. Pepper* had come out, but the scene in the Village still had an earnest and folky vibe. Michael and Chris's songs reflected that. With titles such as "These Are My Children," "Carol Arrives," "Hello, Isabel," "Castle by the Sea," and "Bacon Billy Roe" (about a Civil War drummer boy), they had "earnest" written all over them.

Chris was a genuine product of the world he would later satirize in his terrific 2003 film, *A Mighty Wind*. He grew up in Greenwich Village in the 1950s and '60s. His father, Peter Haden-Guest, was an English diplomat and member of the House of Lords who worked at the United Nations. His mother, Jean, was a casting director who later became one of the first female executives at CBS. One of Chris's childhood babysitters was Mary Travers, later of Peter, Paul and Mary. Chris took up the guitar and mandolin in his teens, but his first instrument was the clarinet, which he studied at Manhattan's High School of Music & Art. While there, he played in a band called Ziggy Muldoon with a fellow student named Michael Kamen, the future composer and conductor.

The timing of Ziggy Muldoon's one and only gig was inauspicious. "It was at either the Pierre or the Sherry-Netherland," says Chris. "The date was Friday, November 22, 1963. I took the subway up with my instrument, got to the hotel ballroom, and it was empty. A guy was sweeping up. He said, 'Can I help you guys?' We said, 'We're the entertainment for tonight.' He said, 'Have you turned on the TV?'

This is the mind of a fifteen-year-old: I thought, why would the assassination of President Kennedy have anything to do with our gig?"

Music & Art proved a bit too classical for Chris, who, as he will tell you, had neither the desire nor the ability to become a concert clarinetist. So he spent his junior and senior years at the Stockbridge School, a boarding school in western Massachusetts. There, he befriended an upperclassman named Arlo Guthrie, whose father, the folk legend Woody Guthrie, was suffering from Huntington's disease and nearing the end of his life. Says Chris, "Arlo was not known at that time. But I was a big Woody Guthrie fan and I was aware that Arlo was his son. I was already in a band and said to Arlo, 'It would be cool to play together. I have a guitar.' He said, 'I have a guitar, too, but I'll tell you what: I'll give you *this*.' He handed me a mandolin. 'This was my dad's,' he said.

"I actually thought, 'Oh, fucking great. I'm going to catch that disease, touching this thing.' That was how scientifically astute I was.

"I started playing with Arlo. One of the places we played was the Austen Riggs Center, where James Taylor was later institutionalized. We were invited to play for people who were on lithium. They were all listing to one side, eyes glazed, and there was a guy coming around with a rag to wipe their mouths. They didn't react to anything we played—no applause, nothing. I thought, 'What the hell?' But the person from the institute very kindly said, 'Thanks for coming, fellas,' and put us on a bus back to our school."

**M**ichael grew up in Sea Cliff, New York, on the North Shore of Long Island. His mother, Ruth, was a librarian, and his father, Gilbert, worked at a series of record companies. Gil McKean was not, as the internet insists, a founder of the British label Decca Records.

What is true is that he worked briefly at Decca after having been stationed in London as a member of the U.S. Army Signal Corps. This proved to be a boon for Michael. "My dad met a lot of people who were connected to the jazz world," he says. "He loved listening to jazz and decided he wanted to write about jazz for a living. So he started writing profiles of jazz musicians for *Downbeat* and *Esquire*. He sold Dictaphones for a while, then got jobs at Columbia Records and RCA Victor, mostly doing editorial writing."

Immersed in music, Michael had an enviable collection of records that, thanks to his father, he was able to get for free. He was also blessed with the rare set of parents who were not horrified that their child wanted to pursue a life in acting and music.

Though Michael's time at Carnegie Tech was brief, in his one year there he made some lasting friendships: with a future short-term Spinal Tap member, Loudon Wainwright III, and with a drama major named David Landau. Michael and David had instant chemistry. Within weeks of meeting each other, they started schnadling as a pair of greaser characters named Lenny Kosnowski and Anthony Squigliano. It would be ten years before everyone in America would come to know them as Lenny and Squiggy on the hit ABC sitcom *Laverne & Shirley*.

While Michael and Chris were connecting at NYU, Harry was teaching English and social studies at Compton High School in Los Angeles. Harry grew up in L.A. His father, Mack, owned a Shell gas station in nearby Redondo Beach. Mack died when Harry was only twelve. His mother, Dora, then ran a Texaco station, with Harry helping out by pumping gas and cleaning windshields.

Harry, too, was a musical kid. His parents started him on piano lessons when he was four. This decision improbably led to his career in show business, though not as a musician. As Harry explains, "My piano teacher had a daughter who was a child actress. About two and a half years into teaching me, she decided to change careers and become an agent for children. She called my parents to see if she could 'try to get Harry some work.' The first audition I went on was for *The Jack Benny Program*, and I got it."

That was the beginning of what would be an eight-year stint as a player on Benny's show. Young Harry also appeared on *Alfred Hitchcock Presents*, *Leave It to Beaver*, and *General Electric Theater*. Harry's parents were careful and protected him from becoming a show business casualty. They turned down opportunities for him to work full-time on a series. He stayed in school and attended UCLA as a political science major. After graduation, Harry went through what he calls his "serious phase." He spent a year in grad school at Harvard studying urban government. Then he interned at the California State Legislature in Sacramento before returning to L.A. to teach at Compton High.

Harry's path to unseriousness came through a job in radio. KRLA, the also-ran AM rock station in Los Angeles, had existed forever in the shadow of the more popular KHJ. In their desperation, KRLA decided to take a flyer on comedy. They wanted to try a satirical news show that would air three times a day in ten-minute installments. At that time, Harry had a job buying and creating radio ads for a local music venue. But when a contact at KRLA told him about what the station was planning, Harry recorded a sketch, drove the tape to KRLA's offices in Pasadena, and was hired the following day.

Not long after Harry was hired, Michael's old friend from Carnegie Tech, David Landau, who had de-Jewified his name to David Lander, became part of the satirical news program, which was called *The Credibility Gap*. Richard Beebe, a real newsman, rounded out the team. In addition to performing on KRLA, the Credibility Gap guys played live comedy shows in theaters and clubs.

**M**y beginnings in improvisational comedy started in the basement of Royce Hall at UCLA. I was nineteen and a student there. Along with my future writing partner Phil Mishkin, I formed a group that we called the Session. I directed and acted in a cast that included Richard Dreyfuss and Larry Bishop, the son of comedian and Rat Pack member Joey Bishop. Both Ricky, as I called him back then, and Larry, who was also attending UCLA, had been classmates of mine at Beverly Hills High School.

Like Larry, I, too, had a famous father, Carl Reiner. For the uninitiated, my dad performed with Sid Caesar on *Your Show of Shows*, created *The Dick Van Dyke Show*, directed a number of great film comedies starring Steve Martin, and, with Mel Brooks, recorded the classic *2000 Year Old Man* comedy albums. Comedy was in the air I breathed, and, due to my mother, there was also music.

Estelle Reiner—now best remembered as the woman who says, "I'll have what she's having" after Meg Ryan fakes an orgasm at Katz's Deli in my film *When Harry Met Sally*—was a gifted jazz singer. In her teens, she sang on the radio. But she put aside her musical ambitions to raise me and my siblings, Annie and Lucas. Once we were all out on our own, she took up singing again and performed at the Gardenia club in West Hollywood and at the Algonquin and Carlyle hotels in New York.

I was of the first generation to grow up on rock 'n' roll. I had stacks of 45s by Little Richard, Jerry Lee Lewis, and the Everly Brothers. In the sixties, I worshipped at the altar of Buffalo Springfield, Cream, Joni Mitchell, Janis Joplin, and the Doors. And I had, and still have, a love of the blues. Any chance I got, I'd run to see B. B. King, Albert King, James Cotton, Taj Mahal, Lightnin' Hopkins, or Jimi Hendrix. And being a fallen Jew, I loved Mike Bloomfield. When I saw him play with the Paul Butterfield Blues Band and later with the Electric Flag, I secretly wished I could do what he did. On the guitar, that is.

But my focus was on my improv group, the Session. Every night for six months, we snuck into the basement of Royce Hall to rehearse, until one night the campus police discovered what we were up to and politely kicked us out. But by then, we had managed to put a show together, and, after doing some backers' auditions, we secured our own theater on the Sunset Strip. We also played the Troubadour in West Hollywood and the Playboy Club in New York.

After a year, the company disbanded. Larry and I decided to continue on as a double act. We appeared on *The Steve Allen Show*, *The Mike Douglas Show*, and *The Hollywood Palace*. We also performed in nightclubs. At the famous Hungry I in San Francisco, we opened for jazz singer Carmen McRae. From there, we were booked into Mister Kelly's in Chicago, the Roostertail in Detroit, Paul's Mall in Boston, and the Bitter End in New York.

But after the Hungry I, where we got great reviews, Larry said he wanted to quit. I don't think he liked the idea of following his father's path of playing clubs; he wanted to be an actor. So we canceled the rest of our gigs. I was disappointed, but I understood.

Soon after that, I learned that the Committee, the legendary improv group based in San Francisco, was forming a company that would be based in Los Angeles. When putting the Session together,

I had spent a lot of time up in San Francisco observing and learning from them. I had become friendly with Committee members Howard Hesseman, Carl Gottlieb, Chris Ross, and Leigh French, as well as the group's founder and director, Alan Myerson. So when Alan asked me if I wanted to join the L.A. company, I was thrilled. I was a huge fan of what they did. They weren't just doing social satire, they were also playing in the political arena.

Along with performing in the Committee, for a time in the late sixties I became the resident Hollywood Hippie, getting cast as the long-haired face of youth in sitcoms that were straining to be relevant. I did parts on *The Beverly Hillbillies* and *Gomer Pyle, U.S.M.C.* In the latter, I, along with fellow Committee members Chris Ross (on guitar) and Leigh French (in a granny dress and face paint), joined Jim Nabors's sweet-natured marine in an acoustic rendition of "Blowin' in the Wind." If you're compelled to see it, you can find it on YouTube. I promise, it won't disappoint.

Being part of the Committee was a big deal for me. Not only did it give me a chance to work and learn from great improvisers, it also led to my first job as a writer for television. One night, Tommy Smothers, who was staffing up for a summer replacement show for *The Smothers Brothers Comedy Hour*, came in to see us and ended up plucking me and Carl Gottlieb from the cast to be writers for what he was calling *The Summer Brothers' Smothers Show*. It was to star an up-and-coming singer and guitarist named Glen Campbell. A young comedian named Steve Martin was also hired. Steve and I were the two youngest members on the writing staff, and we were kind of thrown together as a team. They didn't use much of what we came up with, but we did get a couple of pieces on the show. One of them featured the first fart joke ever done on network television. I'm quite proud of that.

My burgeoning writing career also included an ABC special cheesily titled *Romp!!!* It was yet another desperate attempt by a major network to be "happening" and "groovy." The quasi-psychedelic variety show was cohosted by Ryan O'Neal and Michele Lee. There's not much to say about *Romp!!!* except that the writer I worked with on it was a good friend and a really funny guy named David Lander.

Yes, the same David Lander who had gone to college with Michael and was soon to work with Harry as a member of the Credibility Gap.

You can see where all this is headed. But at the time, I don't think anyone would have imagined that Squiggy, of all people, would forge the connections that would make rock 'n' roll history.

CHAPTER 2

# It's Getting Louder Every Day

In the winter of 1970, Michael decided to leave NYU and move west. The previous summer, while acting in a play at a repertory theater in Connecticut, he had met a girl from California. He had also received a call from his Carnegie Tech pal David Lander inviting him to join the Credibility Gap—they needed another writer-performer, and it helped that Michael was also a singer and songwriter.

"So I had two good reasons to go out to California," Michael says. He had saved up money by singing on a series of children's records and briefly working as a guitarist for the Left Banke, a pop act known for their hit songs "Walk Away Renée" and "Pretty Ballerina."

When Michael's plane touched down in Los Angeles, David's then wife, Thea, was there to meet him. His first experience of L.A. was even better than advertised. "Thea greeted me, stuck a lit joint in my mouth, and said, 'Welcome to L.A.,'" Michael says. "I was thinking, 'So far, so good. I'm high as a kite and the weather's perfect.'

"The first month, I stayed at David and Thea's, which was right around the corner from the famous Tropicana Motel on Santa Monica Boulevard. The motel featured a little breakfast place called Duke's Coffee Shop. Everyone went there. You'd walk in and see Jim Morrison, Iggy Pop, Tom Waits. I thought, 'This is, if not paradise, then certainly paradisiacal.'

"One night, David and Thea took me to a folk music club called the Ash Grove. The banjo player Doug Dillard was the headliner. His opening act was a singer-songwriter named Penny Nichols, who also happened to be Harry Shearer's girlfriend. David had told me all about Harry: 'You'll love him. He's great with voices. He does Mayor Sam Yorty and a great Richard Nixon.' I'd heard Harry on tapes that David had sent me and was really impressed. For some reason I was expecting a kind of straitlaced guy in a shirt and tie.

"When our car pulled up to the Ash Grove, Thea said, 'There's Harry.' I said, 'Where? Behind the hippie guy with the long hair and the mattress-ticking pants?' She said, 'No, Harry *is* the hippie guy with the long hair and the mattress-ticking pants.'"

**M**ichael and Harry hit it off, and Michael joined the Credibility Gap alongside David and Richard Beebe. For a couple of years, every weekday, three times a day, the four guys had to come up with fresh material tied to the news of the day. Harry remembers, "We would do the first show in the morning and then go to the Hamburger Hamlet for a lunch break. Then we'd get high and do the second and third shows in the afternoon."

This particular Hamburger Hamlet, in Pasadena, had a peculiar system where, rather than ringing a bell to inform a waitress that her order was ready, the cook would get on a microphone and page her. "There was this one waitress named Betty who the cook could never find," Harry recalls. "Sometimes he'd call for her four or five times: 'Betty, please pick up. Betty, please pick up. Betty, *please*.' So we started writing restaurant sketches just to work 'Betty, *please*' into the show."

Michael continued to write and play music. At the urging of Penny Nichols, he got up the courage to sing on open-mic nights at the Troubadour, a storied music club on Santa Monica Boulevard. The Troubadour is often credited for launching L.A.'s singer-songwriter movement. One night, Michael was followed by a budding songwriter named Jackson Browne.

L.A.'s Laurel Canyon, in the hills above Sunset Boulevard, was *the* place for young creative people during that period. Neil Young, Joni Mitchell, Graham Nash, David Crosby, and Frank Zappa all lived in the canyon. In 1969, I moved into a house there with my then girlfriend and future wife, an actress named Penny Marshall. The future Han Solo and Indiana Jones, Harrison Ford, who at the time was earning money as a carpenter, built bookshelves for us. And through my Committee friend Carl Gottlieb, we got to hang out with Crosby, Young, Steve Miller, and Mama Cass Elliot.

We also became friendly with Janis Joplin, who on occasion would join the Committee onstage. Cass's sister, Leah Kunkel, was married to the man who would become Tap's first drummer, Russ Kunkel. And Leah, when she was still Leah Cohen, had gone to the Stockbridge School in Massachusetts with Chris Guest. Everybody seemed to know everybody.

On a visit to New York, I met Michael for the first time, through David Lander. I also met Chris in New York, when I saw him in the stage show *National Lampoon: Lemmings*. Chevy Chase, John Belushi, and Tony Hendra, who would later play Spinal Tap's manager, Ian Faith, were also in the cast.

In *Lemmings*, Chris did brilliant impressions of Bob Dylan and James Taylor. He and I exchanged hellos after the show but wouldn't really get to know each other until a few years later, when he appeared in an episode of the sitcom I was in, *All in the Family*. The night I saw *Lemmings*, I was also blown away by John Belushi's body-contorting impression of the British blues singer Joe Cocker. When I hosted *Saturday Night Live* in 1975, I suggested to Lorne Michaels that John do his Cocker impression on the show. Lorne liked the idea and John wound up bringing down the house. A year later, Joe Cocker himself appeared on *SNL* alongside John, as Dueling Cockers.

The first-ever episode of *SNL* was hosted by George Carlin, followed by Paul Simon. I was the third host. The reason I was even asked to host was that *All in the Family* had made me a household name. The program was Norman Lear's adaptation of a British sitcom called *Till Death Us Do Part*. Norman transplanted the characters from London's East End to a working-class neighborhood in Queens, New York. Carroll O'Connor and Jean Stapleton were set from the beginning to play Archie and Edith Bunker. But Norman had a hard time finding the right actors to play the Bunkers' daughter, Gloria, and her liberal husband, Mike Stivic.

Two separate pilots were taped for ABC with two different Gloria-Mike pairings. ABC rejected both pilots. Then, in 1970, the show migrated to CBS for a third shot. Penny and I auditioned for Gloria and Mike. Even though Penny and I would become a married couple the following year, Norman thought I had better chemistry with Sally Struthers.

*All in the Family* premiered as a mid-season replacement in January of 1971. Initially, it was met with trepidation and some confusion; CBS ran a big disclaimer before each episode out of concern that the audience would take offense at a show whose main character, Archie Bunker, was a bigot. But by the end of that summer, after CBS aired the first thirteen episodes as reruns, we had become the number one show in America. For five years straight we remained number one, watched by 40 to 45 million people every week.

I was recognized everywhere I went, and since Archie pejoratively referred to my character, Mike, as Meathead, I was regularly greeted by that lovely handle. Even in Mexico, when someone recognized me, they'd yell, "*Cabeza de carne!*" I've often said that I could win the Nobel Prize and the headline would still read "Meathead Wins Nobel."

Chris stayed in New York for much of the 1970s. He started getting acting jobs, so, like Michael, he dropped out of NYU. His first part was in an off-Broadway production of Jules Feiffer's play *Little Murders*, directed by Alan Arkin. Fred Willard and Paul Benedict, both of whom would end up playing parts in *This Is Spinal Tap*, were also in the cast.

In 1970, Chris joined the staff of the *National Lampoon*, a humor magazine that had been launched that year. Its success led to the *Lemmings* stage show, which Chris cowrote. They also had a popular weekly program called *The National Lampoon Radio Hour*, which led to a series of comedy albums. On these and in the stage show, Chris collaborated with the up-and-coming comic talents Bill Murray, Brian Doyle-Murray, Paul Shaffer, John Belushi, Laraine Newman, Chevy Chase, and Harold Ramis.

With another *Lampoon* writer, Sean Kelly, Chris wrote some great musical parodies. One was a James Taylor send-up called "Highway Toes." In that reedy Taylor tone, strumming his Martin acoustic, Chris sang, "Shootin' up the highway on the road map of my wrist / Baby, I just scratched you off my list."

Says Chris, "*Lemmings* was when I realized that I had something to offer musically. I wasn't trying to be Donovan or anything. Michael's a different story. He could have gone either way. He could have made proper solo albums of his own material. I found this thing that worked great for me, which was that I get to play and do comedy. I thought, 'Well, that's my thing.'"

While performing in *Lemmings*, Chris caught the eye of Lily Tomlin, who invited him to come to Los Angeles to be a writer and performer on her new TV special. Chris had barely been in touch with Michael in the intervening years, but his trip to L.A. allowed them to reconnect in an auspicious reunion for the former NYU songwriting partners. "We got together in my apartment and took out some paper straws," says Michael. "We clipped out a little triangle at the end of each one, making them reeds. Then we poked little holes in them, and Chris and I played straw duets."

During this time, we were all accumulating experiences and stories that would later find their way into *This Is Spinal Tap*. Example: When Chris was in L.A., he paid a visit to a friend who was staying at the Chateau Marmont hotel. Chris:

> As I'm waiting there in the lobby, I notice a band checking in: three English musicians and their manager, with Cockney accents. The manager says to one of them, "Where's your bass?"
> 
> "Wot?"

"I said, 'Where's your bass?'"

"Wot?"

"Your bass. Where's your bass?"

"Where is it?"

"Yes."

"I fink I leffit at the airport."

"You leffit there, you nit?"

"Leff wot?"

"Your *bass*, you nit."

"Wot?"

It went on like this forever. I sat there thinking, "Please, never let this end." It was a gift.

Another time, Chris dropped in at Matt Umanov Guitars, a famous shop on Bleecker Street in the Village. He'd been a customer there since 1964. (The Martin acoustic that he used in *Lemmings* had cost him $900, a fortune when he bought it in 1970; Umanov let him pay in installments.) As Chris was shooting the breeze with Umanov, a well-known British rocker walked in.

"He looked, shall we say, a little bit worse for the wear," Chris recalls. "He was wearing leather pants and there was . . . a noticeable bulge in them. A baguette, basically. The guy pointed to a guitar and asked Matt, 'Can I play that?' Matt said to me, 'Oh, God, that's a fifty-thousand-dollar guitar.' He was worried about what might happen because the guy was really high. The guy played the guitar for a while. Fortunately, no damage was done to the instrument. But when he got up to leave, the bulge in his pants had migrated. It was now down around his ankle. Gravity had done its part. So, you know, I filed that away."

After their radio show was canceled in 1971, Michael, Harry, and David decided to take the Credibility Gap on the road. "KRLA literally told us, 'The times are too serious for humor,'" Michael says. Fortunately, they got plenty of bookings at clubs.

One of the Gap's great bits was a takeoff of Abbott and Costello's classic "Who's on First?" routine. Harry played a music promoter trying to explain to a newspaper adman, David, the order in which he wanted three bands to appear. The bands were the Who, the Guess Who, and Yes. Here's an excerpt:

DAVID: Who's on first?

HARRY: That's right.

DAVID, *writing*: That's Right. Ooh, what a nice name.

HARRY: No, that's wrong.

DAVID: That's Wrong.

HARRY: Mr. Hickenlooper? It's not That's Right. It's not That's Wrong.

DAVID: Well, then who's on first?

HARRY: Who's on first.

DAVID: Who *is* on first?

HARRY: Who. Is. On. First.

DAVID: Who?

HARRY: Who.

DAVID: Who?

HARRY: Who!

**DAVID:** I have a suggestion. Why don't we start with the second act and then we'll go back? Okay, who—um, what's the name of the second act?

**HARRY:** Guess Who.

**DAVID:** Uh . . .

**HARRY:** Guess Who!

**DAVID:** Uh, the Dingaling Sisters.

**HARRY:** The Dingaling Sisters?! First of all, they're not even sisters. But more importantly, we're talking about big-time rock 'n' roll: Guess Who!

**DAVID:** I *can't* guess who!

**HARRY:** You don't have to Guess Who!

**DAVID:** Then I *won't* guess who!

**HARRY:** So *don't* Guess Who!

**DAVID:** All right, let's just move on to the third act. Who—will you please tell me the name of the third act?

**HARRY:** Yes.

**DAVID:** Okay, who?

**HARRY:** No, they're on first.

You get the idea.

The Credibility Gap was booked to perform a show in Tucson, Arizona. The unfortunate events that occurred there would ultimately find their way into *Spinal Tap*. The gig had been pitched as a music conference. But it turned out to be a convention for the employees of companies that made the plastic components for cassette tapes. A short, energetic promo man from Warner Bros. Records named Lou Dennis was in charge of the logistics.

The show was a complete disaster. Nothing the Gap had asked for was provided: no PA system, no screen behind which the performers could make quick changes. Worst of all, the conventioneers had been drinking all day and were far more interested in groping each other than watching a comedy show.

"It was the biggest fucking mess you have ever seen," says Harry. "We could barely get through the show. When it was over, Lou Dennis comes up to us, and before we could vent our anger, he goes into this routine: 'Guys, I know. I *know*. It's all my fault. It's me. It's all me. Do me a favor. Kick my ass. *Kick my ass*. I'm not asking you, I'm telling you: *Kick my ass*.'

"We couldn't get angry at him. He'd taken that moment from us. He preemptively asked us to kick his ass."

Ten years later, the poetic words of Lou Dennis would be heard coming from the mouth of Paul Shaffer as the hapless Polymer Records promotions rep Artie Fufkin.

In 1977, *All in the Family* was finally knocked from its number one spot in the ratings by an ABC sitcom called *Happy Days*. The show was created by my wife Penny's brother, Garry Marshall. A year after that, the top-rated show on TV was a *Happy Days* spin-off called *Laverne & Shirley*, another Garry Marshall show. Penny and Cindy Williams starred as Laverne DeFazio and Shirley Feeney, bottle-cappers at the Shotz Brewery in Milwaukee.

When *Laverne & Shirley* was being developed, Penny and I threw a party at our house in North Hollywood. We invited Garry and another of the show's creators, a comedy writer named Lowell Ganz. Penny had this idea that to show off Michael's and David's talents, at an opportune moment, we'd introduce them to Garry and Lowell, and they'd just start riffing as Lenny and Squiggy. It worked. Garry and Lowell were blown away. Michael and David effectively schnadled their way onto the show. Lenny got to keep his Polish last name, Kosnowski. But Squiggy's surname was changed from Squigliano to Squiggman because ABC was worried that the show had too many Italian American characters.

With their somewhat-less-than-genius-level intelligence and Squiggy's patented "*Hell*-o!" entrances, Lenny and Squiggy became household names. The show would occasionally take advantage of Michael's musical talents, giving Lenny and Squiggy a showcase to perform songs.

L.A.'s record company executives took notice. In 1978, John Belushi and Dan Aykroyd had scored a big success with *Briefcase Full of Blues*, an album of R&B and soul standards sung by them as their *SNL* characters the Blues Brothers. When *Briefcase Full of Blues* hit number one on the *Billboard* chart and went double platinum, Neil Bogart of Casablanca Records, the disco-era juggernaut behind the blockbuster albums of Cher, Donna Summer, and the Village People, took one look at Lenny and Squiggy and thought, "The next Blues Brothers!"

Thus was born Lenny and the Squigtones. Michael and David wrote a bunch of fifties- and sixties-style songs for an album called *Lenny & Squiggy Present Lenny and the Squigtones*. It was recorded live at the Roxy Theatre in West Hollywood. The lead single was "King of the Cars," an homage to the Beach Boys . . .

*I've got the fully blown Hemi like the baddest of the street machines*
*And the rearview mirror was imported from the Philippines*

Casablanca booked a tour to support the album, and Michael recruited Chris to join the Squigtones. *Lenny & Squiggy Present Lenny and the Squigtones* failed to burn up the charts, but it musically reunited Michael and Chris.

It also contributed another piece of show business lore that was to prove useful. Casablanca's PR liaison to the band was Bobbi Cowan, a dynamic young woman whose uncle had cofounded the public relations giant Rogers & Cowan.

Bobbi was an enthusiastic supporter of the band, but as the album stiffed and ticket sales for the tour failed to live up to expectations, it was her job to deliver the unvarnished truth—which she did.

"She was really friendly, but she had an abrasive New York accent and weighed about seventy-five pounds," Chris remembers. "She said, 'Fellas, I got some bad news. You're not gonna be flying anymore. You're gonna be driving.' She was basically telling us that tour support was over. That was another one of those stories where we were thinking, 'Is this a character?'"

In this piecemeal fashion, something was starting to take shape. When Lenny and the Squigtones appeared on *American Bandstand*, Dick Clark asked the backup musicians to state their names. Chris, though he had short hair and was wearing a fifties-style red blazer, had already developed his guitar-god alter ego. So, when asked, he nonchalantly replied to Clark, in a working-class English accent, "My name is Nigel Tufnel. I come from Swindon, England, and I play guitar."

## CHAPTER 3

# 'Twas the Rock 'n' Roll Creation

In 1978, after eight years of playing Mike Stivic, I said goodbye to *All in the Family*. I was thirty-one and ready to move on. CBS had other ideas. They would soon offer me a ton of money to do a Gloria-and-Mike spin-off series with Sally Struthers.

But I wanted to get back to what I had been doing. I had already worked as a director with my own improv group. Now I wanted to direct films.

But to go from a sitcom actor to a film director was considered undoable. At that time, there was a big chasm in Hollywood between those who worked in television and those who worked in movies. The film people were considered royalty. They looked down on the lowly peasants of TV. Today, actors, writers, and directors easily shuttle between movies and television. But it wasn't until such sitcom alums as Ron Howard, Danny DeVito, Penny Marshall, and I, along with the TV writers Barry Levinson and Jim Brooks, were successfully directing movies in the eighties that these dividing lines were erased.

My chance to direct a film wouldn't come for a few years, but I managed to get a development deal with ABC to create and produce TV shows, a good first step. With my writing partner, Phil Mishkin, I created and starred in a show called *Free Country*, about Eastern European immigrants coming to America at the turn of the century. It ran for only five episodes as a summer replacement show in '78 before it was canceled.

Then came *The TV Show* and Spinal Tap's first appearance. By this time, I knew Harry and Michael pretty well. By a quirk of fate, I'd only just gotten to know Chris better. He was cast opposite me in one of my last *All in the Family* episodes. It was about how Mike and Gloria had first met. In a flashback, Chris appears as Mike's college roommate. He and his girlfriend, played by Priscilla Lopez, set up a double date for Mike and Gloria to meet. As soon as the four of them get together, Chris's and Priscilla's characters quickly leave to get busy, leaving the worldly Mike and the sheltered Gloria alone. In rom-com vernacular, this is known as a "meet-cute."

When Chris, Michael, Harry, and I worked on the *Midnight Special* sketch, it was a fun time in Schnadleville. We made each other laugh tossing around possible names for the band. After considering Jumbo Prawns, Silver Service, Waffles, and Hot Waffles, we settled on Spinal Tap. Perfect—what could be more heavy metal than a painful medical procedure? We also liked the idea that a group of pretentious British rockers would find that somehow poetic.

Unfortunately, very few people saw Tap's debut; *The TV Show* got buried deep in ABC's '79 summer schedule. Michael returned to *Laverne & Shirley* and Chris got a part in Walter Hill's film *The Long Riders*, which featured four sets of real-life brothers—James and Stacy Keach; Dennis and Randy Quaid; David, Keith, and Robert Carradine; and Chris and his brother Nick—playing the James-Younger Gang.

Harry and I went off to write a movie. We had this idea to do a film about roadies, the guys who set up and break down a rock band's equipment as they travel from city to city. We were less than a week into writing the script when we learned that a movie called *Roadie*, starring Meat Loaf, was already in production. So we folded that tent.

Then Chris was approached by a producer named David Jablin, who was looking for young writers and directors to create comic short films for a cable anthology series he was putting together called *Likely Stories*. Cable television was in its infancy, and *Likely Stories* would only be available on an obscure new subscription-television service called ON TV. Still, Jablin was offering something that the studios weren't: a chance for first-time directors.

Chris hooked me up with Jablin, and my friend Bruno Kirby and I wrote a script for *Likely Stories* called *Tommy Rispoli: A Man and His Music*. Bruno played Tommy, a Sinatra-obsessed limo driver who bends the ear of his New Year's Eve passenger, Rob Reiner, played by Rob Reiner (typecasting). As I sat in the back of the car, Tommy held forth on *All in the Family* ("They shoulda never killed off Edith. You don't kill an institution") and Frank Sinatra ("Frank had loved and lost. But the thing is, he lived to love again. And that's the essence of a great man"). Tommy Rispoli didn't yet know it, but one day, renamed Tommy Pischedda, he would have the distinct privilege of chauffeuring Spinal Tap.

Harry wrote and directed a seven-minute film for *Likely Stories* called *The Making of "You Won't Believe Our World!"* It was a behind-the-scenes look at the making of an industrial film for a multinational conglomerate called Majesco Industries. Playing themselves, Michael and Marcia Strassman, of *Welcome Back, Kotter* fame, are hired to perform the company's upbeat promotional songs (written by Harry and Paul Shaffer) about tuna canneries, farm equipment, and warheads. Harry appears briefly as a self-serious Majesco executive. Chris plays a director-choreographer named Chip "Reno" DiMentibella, who later morphed into *Waiting for Guffman*'s Corky St. Clair.

Chris contributed a black-and-white film noir piece called *Dead Ringer*, a send-up of Raymond Chandler detective movies. He played all the characters, including the women. He made another short for *Likely Stories* that didn't make the cut. It was about a pair of British rockers (Chris and Michael) who run into each other in the lobby of a hotel, and, addled by drugs and general dumbness, can't recall whether or not they played in a band together. It was essentially an extension of the characters they had created for *The TV Show*.

Though the film never aired, Chris showed it to me and I loved it. From there, things just started coming together. What if we took the British rock star characters that Chris, Michael, and Harry had created for *The TV Show* and combined them with the idea Harry and I had for a movie about a rock 'n' roll tour—but instead of focusing on the roadies, we'd focus on the band? We all thought that this could be cool.

So I took the idea to a producer named Martin Starger, who I'd gotten to know when he was the head of ABC. He was now running a production company called Marble Arch, owned by the British media impresario Sir Lew Grade. I told Starger that we wanted to do a satire of rock documentaries. It would be a mash-up of *The Last Waltz*, Martin Scorsese's film about the Band's star-studded farewell concert; Led

Zeppelin's *The Song Remains the Same*; the Who documentary *The Kids Are Alright*; and D. A. Pennebaker's Bob Dylan documentary, *Don't Look Back*.

Starger liked the idea and agreed to pay us $60,000 to write the screenplay. The deal did not include an office, so we met in my room at the L'Ermitage hotel on Burton Way in Beverly Hills. Penny and I had recently separated, and at the time, L'Ermitage was known as the place where newly uncoupled men went to lick their wounds (and possibly other things). In the snug confines of my "bachelor pad," the four of us started working on the script. Harry did all the typing because he was the only one of us who knew how to type.

The choice to make the band English was a natural extension of Chris's being half-English. His father, Peter Haden-Guest, had been a British official at the UN for thirty years, and though Chris normally spoke like an American, his British accent was perfect. He had first used the Nigel accent on the *National Lampoon* album *Goodbye Pop 1952–1976*, in which he played a character named Sid Gormless, the leader of a prog-rock group called the Dog's Breakfast. (In England, the expression "a dog's breakfast" is used the way Americans use "a hot mess.")

But well before that, Chris had been playing around with a version of this accent, having spent his childhood summers with his father's family in England. Chris explains: "My dad was English, but he didn't have a Nigel accent. Nigel has what is now called an Estuary accent, which covers about a hundred square miles around London. When I was a kid, though, it was still a Cockney accent, very much concentrated in the East End. That version of the East End doesn't really exist anymore, but at the time Nigel was growing up there, he would have been a full-blown Cockney. There's an ancient pump in

London called the Aldgate Pump. They say that if you're from east of there, you're a true East Ender. I spent time walking those streets and loved the way the people sounded.

"It also became hip in the sixties and seventies for educated people to adopt working-class accents. Mick Jagger is a good example. He was a middle-class kid who went to the London School of Economics, but *tawked loik dat*. I was fascinated—I thought, 'Well, this is different.'

"If you have something of an ear, you pick up on things like this. It's like music. It *is* music, really. The same was true of *The Goon Show*, the radio show with Peter Sellers, Spike Milligan, Harry Secombe, and Michael Bentine. The voices they did were as pleasurable to hear as a good song. I still do voices when I'm alone in the car. I pick a voice to talk in. It's almost the same level of satisfaction I get from playing guitar."

In my L'Ermitage digs, we worked out the specifics of each band member's character. Michael saw David as the preening frontman, his leonine hair owing more to Peter Frampton, who was huge at the time, than to Robert Plant. "I always wanted him to be named David," he says, "but it was Chris who came up with 'St. Hubbins.' It was funny and we went with it."

Nigel Tufnel was the guitar hero. His name, first floated in that *American Bandstand* appearance with the Squigtones, "was probably a subliminal thing," says Chris. "Some of my family's oldest friends lived in Tufnell Park, which is not spelled the same way, but it's a neighborhood in North London."

Harry came up with the name Derek Smalls, choosing that surname because in the UK, "smalls" is a slang term for underwear. Unlike Michael and Chris, he had rarely played music in public, apart from playing bass on a few dates accompanying his girlfriend Penny.

"I picked up the bass because that's where my ear went when I listened to music," he says.

Derek's soft-spoken presence was a reflection of the "quiet one" position that bassists like John Entwistle and Bill Wyman held in the Who and the Rolling Stones, respectively. "You can track this by the amount of jokes about bass players versus lead guitarists," says Chris. "What happens when a bass player falls out of a plane at thirty-five thousand feet? *Who cares?*"

Or as Derek would later explain in the film, David and Nigel were "like fire and ice, and I feel my role in the band is to be kind of the middle of that. Kind of like lukewarm water."

For my character, I initially chose the name Marty DiBroma, a composite of the names of several directors I admired: Martin Scorsese, Vittorio De Sica, and Brian De Palma. But ultimately, I settled on DiBergi. I lost De Palma, but added Ingmar Bergman and Federico Fellini. But Brian would still get his due. I appropriated his signature safari-jacket-worn-over-a-polo-shirt look.

**T**o steep ourselves in the world of heavy metal, we went on field trips. On June 3, 1980, the four of us drove down to the Long Beach Arena to see Judas Priest, who were promoting their album *British Steel*. All I came away with from that concert was that the band was so loud that I could feel the intense pounding of the bass and drums in my chest. I thought I was having a heart attack.

Harry happened to be visiting England when the hard-rock band Saxon was touring. He persuaded the band to let him tag along as a sort of embedded observer. "I thought it would help to see a quote-unquote real band play larger venues, to see if I could cop any moves off of them," Harry says. "Their bass player was playing open-string E and A and D chords, which allowed him to pump his left fist in the air to the rhythm of the music. So that's the move I copped."

Chris, Michael, and Harry later caught AC/DC on their *Back in Black* tour. This time, they had VIP passes that allowed them to wander the backstage area. "We'd just absorb little things," says Chris. "Like, they had a huge wall of Marshall amps, but if you walked behind them, they were not all plugged in. There might be just a Fender twenty-watt amp back there that was mic'd. But they needed that wall of amps to project power to the audience. I remember thinking, 'Oh!'"

As detailed as the characters had become, and as productive as our fact-finding missions were, we struggled to make the screenplay work. We eventually realized that there was no way we could communicate, in written form, the fly-on-the-wall documentary feel we wanted the film to have. So I went to Martin Starger and asked him to let us use the $60,000 he was paying us for the screenplay to make part of the film. I told him we'd shoot it like a real documentary and give him a sense of what the movie would be like. When he agreed, we were thrilled. It was uncharted waters, but hey, we were going into production!

## CHAPTER 4

# Trying to Raise Some Hard Love

The demo reel's working title was *Rock 'n' Roll Nightmare*, named after the song Tap had performed on *The TV Show*. By the time we started shooting, we had written rough versions of the songs "Tonight I'm Gonna Rock You Tonight," "Heavy Duty," "Big Bottom," "Sex Farm," and "Stonehenge," which we had already imagined as an onstage debacle involving dwarves and an undersized Stonehenge monument. We thought, what could be better than a heavy metal band's pretentious take on the mystery of Stonehenge?

There were other elements of the future feature film already in place. We had Bruno Kirby as the overly chatty limo driver (his chauffeur's sign at the airport originally read SPINE TAPE, later changed to SPINAL PAP). There was a black-and-white sequence showing Tap in an early incarnation as the Thamesmen, and we had Derek setting off the airport metal detector due to a foreign object lodged in his trousers.

These bits added up, and it quickly became clear that our $60,000 budget wouldn't be enough. So I kicked in $25,000 of my own money, and the other three guys together chipped in another $5,000. For $90,000, we put together a twenty-minute demo reel that included interviews, backstage scenes, and onstage performances. We renamed it *Spinal Tap: The Final Tour* and added an umlaut over the *n* in *Spinal* as a nod to Motörhead and Blue Öyster Cult. We placed the umlaut over a consonant as a nod to Tap's stupidity.

Shot in six days at a variety of locations, the demo reel was a manic exercise in guerrilla filmmaking. We ended up with way more material than we could use, so I crammed a bunch of clips into a montage near the end. There is a blink-and-you'll-miss-it appearance by Richard Belzer as the original Artie Fufkin, not only saying, "Kick my ass," but dropping his pants to actually show it. (Paul Shaffer, the ultimate Artie, kept his pants up. He said he would waive the no-nudity clause in his contract if he got paid more. We were on a tight budget, so the world was denied the pleasure of feasting on the Shaffer tush.) You can also see a glimpse of a young Rebecca De Mornay as a groupie in a hot tub with David. And there's a turn by Chris's dad, Peter Haden-Guest, as a fish-out-of-water, bow-tied piano tuner among the long-haired roadies.

We wound up eighty-sixing two planned "as himself" appearances: one by Jeff "Skunk" Baxter from Steely Dan and the Doobie Brothers, the other by Rodney Bingenheimer, the elfin KROQ deejay and Sunset Strip fixture. We also cut a restaurant scene featuring Lorna Patterson, best known as the singing stewardess in *Airplane!*, as an overly solicitous waitress.

Two segments that we shot for the demo reel would make their way into the final film. One was an interview outside a concert venue with a woman listed in the credits as "Ethereal Fan." Her actual name is Jean Cromie, and she was the girlfriend and future wife of Timothy B. Schmit, the Eagles' bassist. Jean had the right look for what we were after: slender, spacey, and blond. She improvised a perfect bit of in-the-clouds ethereal gibberish: "It's like you become one with the guys in the band. The music just unites the people with the players."

The other segment that appeared in the final film was the archival footage of Tap as the Thamesmen, on an early-sixties-type UK program called *Pop, Look & Listen*, performing their minor hit "Gimme Some Money." To give it an authentic vintage feel, we built a set with a musical-staff mural as a background and a checkerboard floor.

Further adding to the authenticity, "It's the only time in the movie when you see everyone's real hair," notes Michael. "When we started talking about doing the demo reel, *Laverne & Shirley* had wrapped for the season and I didn't get a haircut over the summer. Then there was a SAG-AFTRA strike, so I just kept growing my hair."

Instead of the Lenny Kosnowski greaser look, Michael showcased his blond tresses in a blow-dried mod cut modeled on the Yardbirds' Keith Relf. Chris, whose hair was fairly short, simply combed it forward. His motivation was simple. "The Monday after the Beatles played on *Ed Sullivan* for the first time, half of the male student body of every school combed their hair forward as if to say, 'I'm a Beatle now,'" he explains. "Though I like to think of mine as a variation on the Beatles, more Paul Revere and the Raiders or Gerry and the Pacemakers."

The Thamesmen's drummer, the ill-fated John "Stumpy" Pepys, who would die in a bizarre gardening accident, was our good friend Ed Begley Jr. Ed was an unmissably tall, blond, omnipresent L.A. dude. With a pair of geeky glasses, he nailed that nerdy look that some guy in nearly every British beat group had, whether it was Peter Asher of Peter & Gordon or Derek "Lek" Leckenby of Herman's Hermits.

On bass, as Ronnie Pudding, Derek Smalls's predecessor, was the great guitarist Danny Kortchmar. Danny was part of the same L.A. musical mafia as Russ Kunkel and Lee Sklar. Conveniently, for our purposes, he had just been to the barber. Says Danny, "The costume for all of the 1970s had been the dirty Zildjian T-shirt with jeans that didn't fit and fucked-up long hair. I decided that no longer looked right. So I had just gotten a short, Beatles-style haircut. I guess word got out."

Getting Tap's metal-era hairstyles right for the demo reel proved challenging. Chris's pageboy wig came pretty close to the look Nigel ended up having, but Harry's stringy black wig had been glued onto his scalp without the mercy of a bald cap. It took him hours in the bathtub to get the thing off without yanking out his real hair. And Michael's wig wasn't the shaggy, textured mane later associated with David St. Hubbins; he sported a glamorous curtain of straight blond hair that covered half his face. "I looked like Veronica Lake—or, more honestly, Gena Rowlands," he says.

**W**hen the reel was finished, we felt that in those twenty minutes, we had done what we wanted to do: satirically portray all the clichéd elements of a rock documentary. It was close to the bone, but just skewed enough to be funny. I delivered the reel to Martin Starger along with a four-page bible we'd written detailing Spinal Tap's history, from their skiffle days to the controversy over the cover of their latest album, *Smell the Glove*. We eagerly awaited his response.

We didn't have to wait long. It came swiftly and definitively. Something along the lines of "What the fuck is this?"

Taking that as the "No" it was intended to be did not make us a happy group of boys. Starger's reaction just confirmed the old theater adage with which we were all too familiar: satire is what closes on Saturday night. Still, we believed in our idea and took the bad news in stride. That is, if internally screaming, "Fuck you, Starger" qualifies as "in stride."

Marble Arch wrote off its $60,000, and we, now armed with our twenty-minute demo reel, decided to invade enemy territory: Hollywood.

CHAPTER 5

# Pound Notes, Loose Change, Bad Checks, Anything

After Starger's "Don't let the screen door hit you on the way out" dismissal, my producing partner, Karen Murphy, and I hustled to set up meetings at any studio that would see us. Karen had a background in documentaries and had worked on a few projects with Harry, including his contributions to the *Likely Stories* series. She'd also briefly dated Chris. Karen got what we were doing and was willing to take on the thankless task of producing our uncharacterizable film. She would later go on to produce all of Chris's mockumentary films.

But at the time, Karen and I were babes in the Holly-woods. We had no script, just the twenty-minute demo reel in a metal film can, which I literally carried under my arm to each meeting. I remember saying to Karen, "If this movie ever gets made, we'll have the classic story of going from studio to studio schlepping a can of film."

As a Jew, you always hope for the best, but expect the worst. My heritage didn't disappoint.

"It wasn't that hard to set up the meetings," Karen says, "because Rob was a well-known actor in Hollywood. Everybody loved meeting the Meathead. But Rob as a director? That was another story. We kept it super cheerful. We literally laughed at ourselves one day, walking through yet another Hollywood studio parking lot. The temperature was in the nineties and I said to Rob, 'This is what the Avon lady goes through. You're going to someone's door to sell them something they're not even sure they want, but you have to be so enthusiastic and happy about it that they'll buy it.'"

The trouble was that, for all our Avon lady enthusiasm, no one was buying. "When we did our pitch to executives, the look on their faces was so blank," says Karen. "I don't think they knew what heavy metal music was. And we were selling a *comedy* about heavy metal music. That really confused them. They were polite and curious enough, but they had no grasp of what we were pitching."

Every single studio turned us down. Most of the executives didn't even bother giving us a reason. One of the few who did was the controversial David Begelman, who had notoriously been ousted from Columbia Pictures after it was discovered that he had embezzled money from the studio and forged a check in the name of the actor Cliff Robertson. But the embezzler had rebounded, and, in the time-honored Hollywood tradition, was bigger than ever. Begelman was now the head of MGM.

"Begelman didn't even get all the way through the reel," says Michael. "He just said to us, 'Boys, I'll be honest with you. I've already given the Eagles a million dollars to make a movie.' Of course, no such movie was ever made. But it was worth the price of admission just to hear David Begelman say the words 'I'll be honest with you.'"

The string of rejections added to an already rough time in my life. I was going through a divorce from Penny, and my dream of directing a film had all but disappeared. Still, I kept busy. I wrote a TV movie with Phil Mishkin called *Million Dollar Infield*, based on a then-unpublished novel by Dick Wimmer. It was about a group of guys in their thirties who struggle with personal and professional issues, finding their only moments of happiness on a softball field. Chris and Bruno were in the movie with me. In real life, all of us, along with Billy Crystal, played together on a softball team called the Coney Island Whitefish. For the uninitiated, the name refers to a discarded item, used to prevent conception, that one might encounter floating in the waters off Coney Island.

But I digress. While I busied myself with other pursuits, I had no idea that people around town had seen and liked our twenty-minute reel. I don't know if this is true, but when John Belushi died, Karen heard that among the things they found in his bungalow at the Chateau Marmont was a pirated copy of *Spinal Tap: The Final Tour*.

One person definitely *did* screen the reel, and he would ultimately be responsible for turning everything around. His name was Peter Turner, an agent at the William Morris Agency. At the time, I didn't know him; I wasn't a William Morris client. But unbeknownst to me, Turner brought my name up as a possible director to a young executive who was developing a romantic comedy at an independent film studio called Avco Embassy Pictures. The young executive was Lindsay Doran.

The romantic comedy was written by one of Turner's clients, the screenwriter Phil Alden Robinson, who later went on to achieve great success with *Field of Dreams*. Recalls Lindsay, "When Peter said, 'How about Rob Reiner?,' I said, 'What has Rob Reiner ever directed?' Peter said, 'I saw a twenty-minute parody of a rock 'n' roll documentary that he directed. He's looking to expand it into a feature.' I loved the idea right away. I'd seen *Let It Be* fifty times, and *Gimme Shelter* and *Woodstock*. I thought the genre was ripe for parody."

Lindsay reached out to us, so Karen and I arranged a screening of our reel for her. To say that she got what we were doing is an understatement. When the lights came up, I said to her, "Look, I really hope that Avco Embassy makes this movie. But even if they don't, can you come every time we screen this? Because you laughed in all the right places."

We didn't know how much influence Lindsay would have at the studio. At the time we met, her portfolio included two movies based on novelty country songs, *Take This Job and Shove It* and *The Night the Lights Went Out in Georgia*. But Lindsay believed in us and thought she could persuade her boss, Frank Capra Jr., the son of the famous director, to distribute the film—if we could raise some funds.

I learned about a guy named Bill Immerman, whose company specialized in financing low-budget independent films, including *Take This Job and Shove It*. I met with his head of production, Venetia Stevenson, who, like Lindsay, got the concept of our project immediately. Venetia, whose father, Robert Stevenson, had directed *Old Yeller* and *Mary Poppins*, was an English-born beauty. She had been married to Russ Tamblyn and then Don Everly of the Everly Brothers. Despite our age difference—she had nine years on me—we hit it off and went on a couple of dates. Our romance didn't go anywhere, but our business relationship did. She persuaded Immerman to give us a million dollars.

Everything seemed to be falling into place. We had money and distribution. But just as we were about to go into preproduction, Avco

Embassy changed hands. The new owners, Norman Lear and his business partner, Jerry Perenchio, bought the company and renamed it Embassy Pictures. And as is often done when a film company changes hands, they wiped the slate clean and scrapped every project that Avco Embassy had in development, including ours.

I was beyond disappointed. I had a close relationship with Norman, but business, as they say, is business, and they weren't going to make an exception for me. In my desperation, I reached out to Alan Horn, who was Embassy's new head of business affairs and someone I knew from my *All in the Family* days. I pleaded with him for a meeting with Norman and Jerry.

Alan agreed to set it up. On the day of the meeting I was ushered into a conference room with Norman, Jerry, Alan, and a number of other Embassy executives, including Lindsay, who was the only person from Avco Embassy to have survived the regime change. With no pleasantries exchanged, I launched into an insane, evangelical pitch. My arms were flailing. Steam was coming out of my ears: "You're making a big mistake! If you don't make this movie, you're making a big mistake! You want to get young people into the theater? This will do that. It's got rock 'n' roll. It's funny. They'll go back to see it. Repeat business. You want to keep making the same shit? This is *original*. And it's going to be *huge*. You have to make this! If you don't, you better keep an eye on your firstborn."

Okay, I didn't say that last part, but I screamed everything else. Then I walked out.

I later learned that after I left, Norman looked at everyone in the room and said, "Who's going to tell him he can't do it?" He then told Lindsay to let me know that *This Is Spinal Tap* was a go.

When I got the news, I was ecstatic. I don't know if it was because

I had lost hope that the movie would ever happen or that I was simply so tired of being alone. I was so overwhelmed with feelings for Lindsay that I wanted to propose marriage to her. I settled for giving her a gushing thank-you. When I let the guys know, they, too, wanted to marry Lindsay.

**I**n November of 1982, with a budget of just over $2 million, we were set to shoot *This Is Spinal Tap*. Chris, Michael, Harry, and I spent the spring and summer fleshing out the story, scouting locations, and putting the cast together. We secured a modest office space in the Valley, where we hung up a map charting Tap's U.S. tour stops.

Most of the plot points were already in place. We knew that Spinal Tap's hopes for a hit album would be dashed when Sir Denis Eton-Hogg, the debonair head of Polymer Records and the founder of Hoggwood, a summer camp for pale young boys, objected to their cover for *Smell the Glove*, which showed a scantily clad woman down on all fours wearing a dog collar, with a gloved hand thrust in her face. The bearer of Eton-Hogg's bad news was Polymer's tenacious PR rep, Bobbi Flekman, whose name was an homage both to Bobbi Cowan, Casablanca Records' liaison to Lenny and the Squigtones, and Manny Fleckman, my accountant. Backed into a corner by Bobbi, Tap's manager, Ian Faith, in a sop to the Beatles' *White Album*, consented to go with an all-black cover, bereft of any imagery or text.

Meanwhile, real life continued to provide fodder for the film. We read an article in *Rolling Stone* headlined "The Endless Party." It described Van Halen's absurd contract rider, which, among other things, specified that absolutely under no circumstances were brown

M&M's to be allowed in their greenroom backstage. Our first thought was to have a scene with Ian on the phone, rattling off to a promoter the band's nonnegotiable demands for backstage goodies. In our notes, we wrote, "A case of Heinekens for the band, a case of Coors for the crew, assorted deli platters, a selection of beef sticks, cheese balls, and sherried clam puffs in a crystal server, and four dozen Mr. Goodbars with the nuts removed."

In the end, we decided that a visual would be better. So we had Chris, as Nigel, complain about the discrepancy between miniature slices of bread and regular-sized cold cuts. Chris was brilliant, venting to Ian about the indignity of it all. But as a "professional," Nigel promised, he would "rise above it."

We were handed another perfect idea by John Sinclair, who was Tap's keyboard player in our demo reel. John was a great musician who was authentically English and rock star handsome. But he didn't have the luxury of waiting around to see if we were ever going to get the film made. So while we were in limbo, he accepted an invitation to join Uriah Heep, a hard-rock UK band that was touring its new album, *Abominog*. Even though we ended up using a lot of John's keyboard tracks on the soundtrack album, we hired another British keyboard player, David Kaffinetti, formerly of a prog-rock band called Rare Bird, to play Viv Savage in the film. Visually a combination of all three of the Stooges, Kaffinetti was more of a comic presence than a heartthrob, which was fine.

But we kept in touch with John Sinclair. And in one of his check-ins with Chris, he recounted an episode that would make a perfect addition to Tap's long list of humiliations.

Like Tap, Uriah Heep was past its commercial prime and playing in smaller venues than before. As John recalls, "We had a gig canceled.

We were on such a tight budget that our tour manager filled the date with a gig at an air force base, just to keep some dough coming in to cover tour-bus rentals, hotels, and so forth. When we arrived at the base, we were slightly perturbed to see a bright Day-Glo poster with glitter on it that said something like 'The Uriah Heep Show. Over 100 Million Records Sold. Second Only to ABBA in Popularity!'

"When it was time for the show, we were confronted with an audience of guys in full uniform accompanied by wives and girlfriends in their best evening dresses. From the initial slamming metal riff of 'Sell Your Soul' to the slamming metal riff of 'Gypsy' at the end, there was silence. We died a dramatic death."

This *had* to be in the film. So we came up with a scene where, after Tap's original gig in Seattle gets canceled, they are rebooked at an air force base—the perfect setting for "Sex Farm," with its romantic lyrics of "Plowing through your bean field / Planting my seed."

This also gave us the opportunity for Nigel's guitar heroics to be ruined by radio interference and military cross-chatter bleeding through his guitar pickup. The germ of this idea came in the summer of '82, when Chris attended an outdoor production of Shakespeare's *A Midsummer Night's Dream* in Central Park. "The actors had lavalier mics on," he recalls. "All of a sudden, taxi calls started coming over on them: 'Pick 'er up at Fawty-Fifth Street! Take her ovah to Amsterdam!' The actors didn't know what to do. They were frozen, just standing there, not sure how to go on. Then, just as they resumed saying their lines, a blast of static: '*Bzzzsht!* Go to Amsterdam! *Amsterdam*, I says!' The audience was going insane with laughter. For the actors, it was over. The spell was broken. You can't ever get the audience back because you don't know when it's going to happen again."

In shaping the film, we used note cards that we tacked up on a corkboard. Each card represented a scene in Tap's ill-fated tour. We referred to these cards as Grimsbies. Why, you ask? Isn't it obvious? No? Okay, I'll explain. In Harry's first season on *Saturday Night Live*, he dated a reporter at WABC's *Eyewitness News* named Jane Wallace. Through her, he got his hands on a boxful of cards bearing the headshot of *Eyewitness News*'s stern-looking anchor, Roger Grimsby. The back sides of the cards were blank. Whenever we came up with an idea that we thought could work, we'd say: "Does this deserve a Grimsby?"

If we felt it did, we tacked the card on the board. At any given point in our creative process, if you looked at the board, you might see a Grimsby with the words VISITING GRACELAND or MOKE MAKES DEREK DICKS written on it. Though Roger Grimsby retired in 1991 and died in 1995, the term "Grimsby" survives as an integral part of our creative process. When we started working on the sequel to *This Is Spinal Tap*, Michael, committed to upholding the tradition, had a new set of Grimsbies printed up.

**T**o hone their chops in preparation for *This Is Spinal Tap*, the guys played a handful of local gigs in full hair and wardrobe. "It was not hard for us to get bookings in the types of places we played," says Harry. "Two were on the Sunset Strip and one was out in Huntington Beach, a place called the Golden Bear."

For a brief moment we considered filling out the band with a couple of well-known musicians. We actually had meetings with Paul Stanley of Kiss and John Densmore of the Doors. But ultimately, we decided that known musicians would alter the parallel rock universe we had created for Tap.

So the group that played the live dates was the one that appeared in the film: Michael, Chris, Harry, Dave Kaffinetti on keyboards, and, on drums, Ric Parnell, who was a holdover from the demo reel. Ric was a tall, gangly guy from London with a sweet disposition and an elegantly wasted physical appearance. He was the perfect Mick Shrimpton, the latest in Tap's long line of ill-fated drummers. He was also a terrific drummer who had played in an English band called Atomic Rooster. "He was exactly what we needed," says Michael. "He was always kind of living on the edge, but he held it together and had this lovely, supportive girlfriend with bleached-blond Harpo Marx hair. You can glimpse her a few times in the movie."

The most memorable of Tap's pre-shoot gigs took place at Gazzarri's, a Sunset Strip nightclub that had once featured the Doors as its house band but had devolved into a showcase for minor metal acts and past-their-prime heritage groups. "We were supposed to open for Iron Butterfly," says Michael, "but we unintentionally ended up having them open for us. At the last minute, they came up to us and said, 'Guys, would you mind if we went on first? Our bass player had a dental procedure today and he's not feeling great.' So they ended up playing before us. Of course, they made us sit through an extra-long version of 'In-A-Gadda-Da-Vida.' And someone stole our tuner that night."

The pre-filming gigs proved a success, in that no one in the audiences questioned Tap's validity—the band seemed no different from any number of groups looking to make it as they patrolled the Strip.

As shooting drew closer, I had a concern that if the film didn't have an emotional element to hang things on, it might feel like just a string of funny episodes. This led to what might be called the "Yoko plot," a classic rock trope in which a woman comes between the creative forces in the band. We gave David a headstrong romantic partner named Jeanine Pettibone. The term "New Age" was not yet in widespread use, but Jeanine was as New Age as anyone would become. She was a post-hippie inhabitant of a rock 'n' roll faerie-land where people chanted and consulted astrological charts. But beneath all the peace and love lurked a piranha. Jeanine would wage war not only against Nigel but against Ian, which resulted in his resignation as manager.

Casting Jeanine proved a challenge. We wanted a real Englishwoman who could hold her own with Michael, Chris, and Harry. We auditioned several actresses, among them Anjelica Huston, who, though American, had spent much of her childhood in England and Ireland thanks to the peripatetic wanderings of her father, the legendary director John Huston. Anjelica did her audition in what she calls "an authentic Notting Hill accent." Though she wasn't quite right for the role, I liked her presence and thought she would be great to play Polly Deutsch, the young production designer who delivers the undersized Stonehenge replica to Ian Faith. And she scored perfectly.

We still needed a Jeanine. When June Chadwick came in, she couldn't have been less like the character we had thought of. June was a conservatory-trained cellist and pianist who had graduated from London's Royal Academy of Music and was relatively new to acting. But June kicked ass. She matched the guys schnadle for schnadle.

"I was told to come back for an improv session," June recalls. "I was asked, 'How did you and David meet?' I said, 'Well, I saw him, went backstage, thought he was a bit attractive, and that I'd have a whirl. So he banged me in the bog.'"

June fit right in and was cool with whatever we'd throw at her. We thought it would be funny for her to at some point mispronounce the word "Dolby" as "Dobly." She put that in her back pocket, but we had no idea when or how she would deploy it. June then masterfully served it up during a tense conversation in a diner. As she critiques the mix of *Smell the Glove*, she arrogantly tells Nigel, "You don't do heavy metal in Dobly!"

It also worked that, with June's blue eyes and shaggy blond hair, she looked like Michael in his David St. Hubbins wig, making them the perfect self-absorbed rock couple—so narcissistic that they were in love with their mirror images.

We thought that Michael Palin, of the *Monty Python's Flying Circus* troupe, would be great as Ian Faith. But none of us knew him, and we so revered him that we were too scared to approach him. We all knew Tony Hendra. Chris had worked with him in their *National Lampoon* days. Tony had also made a number of guest appearances on the Credibility Gap's radio show. And before that, he had appeared on *The Ed Sullivan Show* as part of a comedy duo called Hendra and Ullett.

Tony was perfect for the part: a burly guy who had gone to the University of Cambridge but had a menacing, wonky-eyed stare. This lined up with Chris's take of "a guy with a good education behaving as working-class and blue-collar as he could for macho reasons."

To fill out the cast, we called on friends who we knew shared our sensibility and had the requisite schnadling chops. Fred Willard, who played the band's air force liaison, Lieutenant Bob Hookstratten, had also been on the *Sullivan Show* in the sixties, as part of the comedy team Greco and Willard. Michael and Harry knew Fred and admired him from his days with the 1970s improv group the Ace Trucking

Company, which sometimes shared bills with the Credibility Gap. And it didn't hurt that Fred had actually served in the military.

We shot our film at a time when show business parties and events were becoming more elaborate and thematic. So for Tap's tour launch party, we thought it would be funny to have some kind of gimmicky caterer. My good friend Billy Crystal threw out this idea: a catering company staffed entirely by mimes. He would play Morty the Mime, the owner of an outfit called Shut Up and Eat. Morty told Marty about how he got the idea for his business: when he was a boy, his father would yell at him during dinner, "Shut up and eat!"

That exchange didn't make it into the final cut, but there's a great moment where Morty dresses down his slow-moving employees, played by Dana Carvey and Committee member Julie Payne, when he tells them to "Move it" because "Mime is money!" We originally considered Dana, then an unknown, for the part of a nerdy "Tap-head" who loyally follows the band from city to city. We decided not to go with that story thread, but we liked Dana so much that we found a way to work him in.

Harry recommended Paul Shaffer for the part of Artie Fufkin. Harry and Paul had become good friends at *Saturday Night Live*, where Paul played piano in the house band. I also knew Paul. We'd met briefly a few years earlier, when he was part of a Monkees-like made-up band that Norman Lear was developing a series for. It never sold, but by 1982, Paul was the bandleader on David Letterman's hip new late-night show and could match Dave schnadle for schnadle.

We were thrilled when Patrick Macnee, who had played Mr. Steed in the 1960s spy series *The Avengers*, agreed to join our little circus as Sir Denis Eton-Hogg, the stuffy head of Polymer Records. But it turned out that Patrick wasn't comfortable improvising. So he ended up with the only scripted dialogue in the film: a speech we wrote in which Sir Denis welcomes the band to the U.S., concluding with, "And so say all of us, 'Tap into America!'"

Fran Drescher was only twenty-five years old and a relative unknown when she auditioned for the part of Bobbi Flekman. She recalls, "I was doing all-night shoots on a Dan Aykroyd movie called *Doctor Detroit*, so I was a little low-energy when I came in, very relaxed, not nervous at all." Fran was younger and prettier than how we had imagined the character, but as soon as she opened her mouth and her native Queens accent flew out, we knew she was Bobbi.

"I'm good at re-creating the people I grew up with. I can easily slip into that kind of character," Fran says. "When we were shooting the thing, I wore all my own clothes. I did my own hair and makeup in the *farkakteh* little dressing room they gave me." Wise beyond her years and a natural, Fran was the perfect force of nature to put Ian Faith in his place with pronouncements like "Money talks and bullshit walks"—an expression she got from her mother.

The groupies who we see draped on the guys at various points in the movie were mostly women we already knew. Chris knew the actresses Joyce Hyser, whom he had briefly dated, and Lisa Freeman. Lisa originally had a bigger role playing an Ass Caster. This was a character based on the real-life L.A. artist Cynthia Plaster Caster, who was known for making casts of the appendages of rock luminaries like Jimi Hendrix and Eric Burdon of the Animals. We had a scene where Derek and Viv are getting their asses cast, but the world will never have the pleasure or the privilege of experiencing their less-than-big bottoms because, alas, the scene was cut. For additional groupies, we roped in Vicki Blue, who had played bass for the Runaways, and Brinke Stevens, a marine biologist turned pinup turned actress. (A logical progression.)

**B**y the time we were ready to shoot, our four-page bible had grown into a forty-page treatment that bore the title *Heavy Duty: A Rock 'n' Roll Odyssey*. It's a detail-rich document stuffed with more scenes and plotlines than we ever shot, along with some less-than-charitable narrative editorializing. Of the young fans gathered outside a concert venue, eagerly awaiting a Tap concert, we wrote, "Heavily sedated yaks would articulate their love for Spinal Tap more clearly than these people." Of Derek's need to enhance his endowment, we wrote, "We hear Derek consider the possibility that his penis is too small for rock 'n' roll."

There was also mention of a character who we ended up not using, one Roger Cross-White, "an upper-class English rock historian who's too old to be doing this sort of thing for a living and gives the events of Tap's career a sense of history and perspective that even the band members themselves aren't pompous enough to articulate."

As detailed as the treatment was, it wasn't a script. We knew what we wanted to have happen in each scene—but all the dialogue would be improvised.

# CHAPTER 6

# Just Want to Make Some Eardrums Bleed

The only parts of the film that were written in advance of shooting, apart from Patrick Macnee's speech, were the songs. Several of them existed in partially realized form thanks to the demo reel, but completing them for the shoot was a challenge. Spinal Tap's repertoire was the cumulative result of years of songwriting. "There was no one process in writing the songs," says Chris. "We wrote in different combinations. I wrote a couple of songs with Harry. I wrote a bunch with Michael. Michael wrote some songs by himself. And some were all four of us."

Now, for you Tapheads out there, the stories behind the songs . . .

### "Heavy Duty"

This lumbering ode to mindless rock—"Just crank that volume to the point of pain / Why waste good music on a brain"—was a Michael McKean song originally written for Lenny and the Squigtones. "David

Lander sang it in performance," he recalls, "and we were going to release it as a single if sales of the Squigtones album warranted further product. But that didn't happen. So it was something I had sitting around."

It was Chris's idea to insert a musical quote from Luigi Boccherini's 1771 String Quintet in E Major, Op. 11, No. 5 into the song. "I listen to and play a lot of classical music at home," he explains. "Sometimes I'll record a section of Vivaldi's Mandolin Concerto for myself. So things like the Boccherini minuet pop into my head. The idea of playing that in a rock style amused me. The same thing happened with the quote from *Eine Kleine Nachtmusik* after the line 'It's like a Mozart symphony' in '(Listen to the) Flower People.'"

Our original plan was to have the band perform "Heavy Duty" before a college crowd at the University of North Carolina, on a stage that still contained the set for the school production of Neil Simon's *Come Blow Your Horn*. The sheer volume of Tap's playing was supposed to make the chandelier from the set shatter and rain glass all over Mick Shrimpton. But we decided not to finish off Mick that soon and in that way.

> *No light fantastic ever crosses my mind*
> *That meditation stuff can make you go blind*
> *Just crank that volume to the point of pain*
> *Why waste good music on a brain*
>
> *Heavy (heavy)*
> *Duty (duty)*
> *Heavy duty rock 'n' roll*
> *Heavy (heavy)*

*Duty (duty)*
*Brings out the duty in my soul*

*I see you dancing there in front of the band*
*You're playing no solos with no guitar in your hand*
*I don't pull no punches, I wouldn't waste your time*
*And just 'cause it pays, that ain't no crime*

*Heavy (heavy)*
*Duty (duty)*
*Heavy duty rock 'n' roll*
*Heavy (heavy)*
*Duty (duty)*
*Brings out the duty in my soul*

*I don't need a woman, I won't take me no wife*
*I got the rock 'n' roll and that'll be my life*
*No page in history, baby, that I don't need*
*I just want to make some eardrums bleed*

*Heavy (heavy)*
*Duty (duty)*
*Heavy duty rock 'n' roll*
*Heavy (heavy)*
*Duty (duty)*
*Brings out the duty in my soul*

## "Tonight I'm Gonna Rock You Tonight"

This catchy, sex-drenched rocker, featuring the cancellation-defying line "You're too young / And I'm too well hung," was entirely Michael's. It's the first song Tap is seen performing in the film.

"We needed an opening number," Michael explains. "We wanted it to be a sexual brag song: 'Boy, are you really gonna wet yourselves tonight.' I couldn't come up with a bridge, so we just had that lingering, vamping section, which actually worked out well because it allowed Rob to introduce each player in the band."

*Little girl, it's a great big world*
*But there's only one of me*
*You can't touch, 'cause I cost too much*

*But tonight I'm gonna rock you (Tonight I'm gonna rock you)*
*Tonight I'm gonna rock you (Tonight I'm gonna rock you)*
*Tonight!*

*You're sweet but you're just four feet*
*And you still got your baby teeth*
*You're too young and I'm too well hung*

*But tonight I'm gonna rock you (Tonight I'm gonna rock you)*
*Tonight I'm gonna rock you (Tonight I'm gonna rock you)*
*Tonight*
*Oh, yeah!*

*You're hot, you take all we got*

*Not a dry seat in the house*
*Next day, we'll be on our way*

*But tonight I'm gonna rock you (Tonight I'm gonna rock you)*
*Tonight I'm gonna rock you (Tonight I'm gonna rock you)*
*Tonight!*

*Little girl, it's a great big world*
*But there's only one of . . .*
*Me!*

## "Big Bottom"

The most enduringly popular Spinal Tap song, "Big Bottom" began at my suggestion. I'd come across the phrase "The bigger the cushion, the better the pushin'" somewhere—on a bumper sticker or a bathroom wall. Michael, meanwhile, had been amused by Queen's double-A-side single "Bicycle Race"/"Fat Bottomed Girls," whose picture sleeve featured an amply buttocked woman atop a bicycle, topless and shot from behind.

"So it was like, 'Yeah, let's write a song about big asses!'" he says. We changed "better" to "sweeter" in the opening couplet, and the rest of the lyrics just flew out of us in a flurry of "big ass" imagery.

It took us a while to find a rhyme for "My baby fits me like a flesh tuxedo." Chris threw out "I want to catch her like Al Gionfriddo." If you're not a baseball nerd, Al Gionfriddo was a Brooklyn Dodgers outfielder who was famous for making a spectacular running catch and robbing the Yankees' Joe DiMaggio of a home run in the 1947 World Series—I would argue a somewhat obscure and not particularly metal reference.

So we temporarily abandoned our usually tried-and-true axiom of "The first stupid idea wins the day" and eventually landed on the far more appropriate "I'd like to sink her with my pink torpedo." Harry came up with the flatulent riff that powers the song, played on a twin-neck bass guitar, or, as he calls it, "the most purposeless instrument of any instrument." Michael and Chris also played basses. The idea of all three guys playing bass on a song called "Big Bottom" was, let's face it, pure heavy metal poetry.

Michael's pseudo-Elizabethan couplet "I met her on Monday / 'Twas my lucky bun day" was indicative of an important motif in Tap songs: pretension. "When we started thinking about the band, pretentiousness was important," says Chris. "It goes back to the imagery in those *Song Remains the Same* scenes: castles and white horses and unicorns. The underlying idea is the guys in the band thinking, 'We are great poets.' So with 'Stonehenge' or 'Rock 'n' Roll Creation,' that was the concept: 'We aren't just making a rock statement but an *artistic* statement.'"

> *The bigger the cushion*
> *The sweeter the pushin'*
> *That's what I said*
> *The looser the waistband*
> *The deeper the quicksand*
> *Or so I have read*
>
> *My baby fits me like a flesh tuxedo*
> *I'd like to sink her with my pink torpedo*

*Big bottom*
*Big bottom*
*Talk about bum cakes*
*My gal's got 'em*

*Big bottom*
*Drive me out of my mind*
*How can I leave this behind*

*I met her on Monday*
*'Twas my lucky bun day*
*You know what I mean*

*I love her each weekday*
*Each velvety cheek day*
*You know what I mean*

*My love gun's loaded and she's in my sights*
*Big game's waiting there inside her tights*

*Big bottom*
*Big bottom*
*Talk about mud flaps*
*My gal's got 'em*
*Big bottom*
*Drive me out of my mind*
*How can I leave this behind*

## "Lick My Love Pump"

This plaintive, wordless piano meditation was something Chris had been noodling with for a while. In the film, Nigel claims that it's part of a larger musical trilogy inspired by Mozart and Bach—"like a Mach piece, really"—and points out that it is played in D minor, "the saddest of all keys." Chris himself more or less agrees with Nigel's assessment, though he asserts that D minor is "battling with A minor to be the saddest."

Michael, however, begs to differ. "Everyone is entitled to have their own saddest key," he says. "I knew a D-flat guy."

## "All the Way Home"

Sitting with Marty in a diner, Nigel and David sing a bit of the first song they ever wrote together. It's the only Tap song with a direct antecedent from a real and specific band: "All the Way Home" is, Michael says, "basically a rewrite of the Beatles' 'One After 909.'" It shares train imagery and a beat with the famous early Lennon-McCartney composition, which didn't surface on record until the release of *Let It Be*, the most Tap-ish of the Beatles' movies.

> *Well, I'm sittin' here beside the railroad track*
> *And I'm waitin' for that train to bring her back*
> *If she's not on the five-nineteen*
> *Then I'm gonna know what sorrow means*
> *And I'm gonna cry, cry, cry*
> *All the way home*

*All the way home (All the way home)*
*All the way home (All the way home)*
*Yes, I'm gonna cry, cry, cry*
*All the way home*

*Well, her daddy never liked me, this he said*
*And he could never get it through his old gray head*
*That I loved his daughter so*
*Did not mean to see her go*
*Now I'm gonna cry, cry, cry*
*All the way home*

*All the way home (All the way home)*
*All the way home (All the way home)*
*Yes, I'm gonna cry, cry, cry*
*All the way home*

*All the way home (All the way home)*
*All the way home (All the way home)*
*Yes, I'm gonna cry, cry, cry*
*All the way home*

## "Gimme Some Money"

Harry was our go-to guy for titles. If we ever got stuck on what to call something, we'd turn to Harry. He came up with "Rainy Day Sun," which became a Kinks-y B-side to "(Listen to the) Flower People." He dubbed Spinal Tap's 1992 comeback album *Break Like the Wind*. And when we needed a song for the young Tap to play as the Thamesmen, Harry suggested "Gimme Some Money."

Michael was the song's main musical architect: "I based the bounce of the song on Elvis Costello's 'Blame It on Cain' and its blues-rock feel on the Yardbirds, especially their version of 'Smokestack Lightning.'"

*Stop wasting my time*
*You know what I want*
*You know what I need*
*Or maybe you don't*
*Do I have to come right flat out and tell you everything?*

*Gimme some money*
*Gimme some money*

*I'm nobody's fool*
*I'm nobody's clown*
*I'm treating you cool*
*I'm putting you down*
*But baby, I don't intend to leave empty-handed*

*Gimme some money*
*Gimme some money*

*(Oh, yeah! Go, Nigel, go!)*

*Gimme some money*
*Gimme some money*

*Don't get me wrong (Gimme some money)*
*Try getting me right (Gimme some money)*
*Your face is okay*
*But your purse is too tight (Gimme some money)*
*I'm looking for pound notes, loose change, bad checks, anything*
*Gimme some money*
*Gimme some money*
*Gimme some money*
*Gimme some money*

## "(Listen to the) Flower People"

According to the bible we created, this 1967 song marked the debut of Spinal Tap as Spinal Tap. The band had cycled through several names since their days as the Thamesmen—including Rave Breakers, Hellcats, Flamin' Daemons, the Doppel Gang, Loose Lips, and the Tufnel–St. Hubbins Group.

"Flower People" was Tap's shameless sop to the sixties psychedelic zeitgeist. It was inspired by what Michael and Chris remembered of 1967's so-called Summer of Love.

"For three months in our lives, everything had the word *flower* in it," Michael recalls. "Scott McKenzie had the song 'San Francisco (Be Sure to Wear Flowers in Your Hair).' There was a top-ten hit in Britain called 'Let's Go to San Francisco' by the Flower Pot Men, a manufactured band of session players who had probably never been to San Francisco. Flower *Pot* Men, get it? Spinal Tap was chasing and jumping on that same bandwagon. And for once, they succeeded and had a surprise hit. It was the only time they ever charted with a single in America."

Ironically, in our bible of Spinal Tap's history, the band's breakthrough hit was not written by Nigel and David. We attributed "Flower People" to bassist Ronnie Pudding, who left the band immediately after the song charted, forming his own band, Pudding People. But Tap's quasi-hit propelled the Pudding-less band to the U.S., where, for their concert and TV appearances, they were joined by Ronnie's replacement, one Derek Smalls, who we said had been a member of "England's pioneer all-white Jamaican showband, Skaface."

*Listen (Shhh)*
*To what the flower people say (Ah-ah-ah-ah-ah-ahhh)*
*Listen*
*It's getting louder every day*

*Listen (Shhh)*
*It's like a bolt out of the blue (Ah-ah-ah-ah-ah-ahhh)*
*Listen, it could be calling now for you*

*Flower people, walk on by*
*Flower people, don't you cry*
*It's not too late (No!)*
*It's not too late*

*Listen (Shhh)*
*It's like a Mozart symphony*
*Listen (Shhh)*
*It's something just for you and me*
*Listen (Shhh)*

*To what the flower people say (Ah-ah-ah-ah-ah-ahhh)*
*Listen, it's getting truer every day*

*Ah-ahhh-ahhhhhhhh*

## "Cups and Cakes"

We wanted a whimsical, quintessentially English song for the B-side of "Gimme Some Money." Once again, Harry threw out a title: "Cups and Cakes." Michael picked up the songwriting gauntlet. "I thought, 'That sounds like a little minuet,' so that's what I wrote: a cute little slice of baroque pop with some violins and shit," says Michael. "Not a whole lot of rock 'n' roll to it. It was another song we credited to Ronnie Pudding. Ronnie was kind of artsy and had pretensions of being a serious musician."

Chris's friend Harlan Collins provided the song's string arrangement. And in a nod to the Beatles' "Penny Lane," a piccolo trumpet was added. (In the sequel to *This Is Spinal Tap*, Paul McCartney makes an appearance, and this "homage" does not go unnoticed.)

*Cups and cakes*
*Cups and cakes*
*Oh, what good things mother makes*
*You've gotta take tea*
*Won't you take it with me*
*What a gay time it will be*

*Cups and cakes*
*Cups and cakes*
*Please make sure that nothing breaks*

The china's so dear
And the treacle so clear
And I'm glad that you are here

Milk and sugar, bread and jam
"Yes please, sir" and "Thank you, ma'am"
Here I am

Cups and cakes
Cups and cakes
I'm so full my tummy aches
How sad it must end
But I'm glad I'd a friend
Sharing cups and cakes with me
And cakes with me

## "Jazz Odyssey"

At the band's lowest point, with Nigel having quit and Jeanine now joining in onstage playing a tambourine, Spinal Tap discovers that its repertoire is suddenly quite limited. Fortunately, the ever-resourceful Derek steps up.

DEREK: I'll tell you what we're gonna have to do.

DAVID: What?

DEREK: "Jazz Odyssey."

DAVID: We're not about to do a free-form jazz exploration in front of a festival crowd.

Cut to Tap in an outdoor bandshell in front of a pathetically small audience.

**DAVID:** You are witnesses at the new birth of Spinal Tap, Mark Two. Hope you enjoy our new direction!

While Chris does not appear in "Jazz Odyssey," he instigated the song's composition, if it can even be called that. "That bass figure that begins it was a jazz figure I had heard somewhere and played," he explains. "Just a modulation in the half-tone. And then the rest is just this . . . sad thing, a jerk-off, as Harry improvises Derek's solo."

## "America"

This adventurous two-parter—Nigel's gentle balladry followed by an explosion of hard rock featuring Derek and David on vocals—is included in full on the soundtrack album, but is heard only fleetingly in the film. Its drum part plays under the load-in scene at the movie's beginning, and it's the song the band is trying to record when Nigel and David erupt into a screaming match in the studio. David struggles to master his guitar part, which irritates Nigel:

**NIGEL:** I hate to cut right to it here. Why don't you play this alone, without some fucking angel hanging over your head, you know what I mean? You can't fucking concentrate because of your fucking wife. Simple as that, awright? It's your fucking wife.

**DAVID:** She's not my wife.

**NIGEL:** Or whatever fuck she is, awright?

We all knew about the legendary *The Troggs Tapes*. It's a widely bootlegged recording of a profanity-laced studio argument between singer Reg Presley and drummer Ronnie Bond, two members of the English band best known for "Wild Thing." Nigel and David's in-studio fight, with support from Derek shouting from the control booth, was our tribute.

Originally, "America" was going to be more prominently featured in the film. We planned to play it under Marty's "cinematic meditation on English musicians experiencing America," including a montage of Tap looking at various symbols of America, like the Lincoln Memorial, the White House, and the Washington Monument, as well as more mundane locations like hamburger stands, a supermarket, and a laundromat. It would end with pastoral footage of the boys running through fields, talking to cows. After which, we'd cut to the band arguing over the song in the studio.

Alas, our budget did not allow for a trip to D.C., let alone a cow pasture. So we went straight for the argument.

Still, in live shows "America" remains a nice showcase for Chris's vocals, along with "Hell Hole" and a song from *Break Like the Wind* called "Clam Caravan." Despite its title, "Clam Caravan" has nothing to do with clams. It was meant to be titled "Calm Caravan," but there was a misprint on the sleeve and by the time the album shipped, it was too late to do anything about it.

> *We came like babies*
> *From our home across the sea*
> *To see America*
> *And the people opened up their arms*

*To welcome us*
*To America*

*We came like children*
*From a far and distant land*
*To see America*
*And the golden sun of freedom*
*Filtered down to us*
*In America*

*And the people stood and stared*
*Loved us more than we had dared to*
*In America*

*Super highways here and there*
*Pretty womens everywhere*
**Brady Bunch** *and* **Smokey Bear**

*Buildings reaching to the sky*
*Afro-sheen and apple pie*
*PTA and FBI*

*Jumbo jet begins to rise*
*A joyful nation waves its bye-byes*

*Each religion, race, and creed*
*Gets exactly what they need*
*God bless Johnny Appleseed*

## "Hell Hole"

The classic rocker's lament: Nigel, singing lead, goes from the gutter to the pinnacle of rock stardom, only to find that the top is no more appealing than the bottom: "The sauna's drafty / The pool's too hot / The kitchen stinks of boiling snails." Therefore, he announces through the song's protagonist, in one of Tap's finest lyrics, "I'm flashing back into my pan."

The melody of "Hell Hole" predated its lyrics. The placeholder title was "Time Code," which is the numeric readout seen on videos used for editing purposes. "The song started with a lick that Chris came up with," Michael says. "'Time Code' was basically a mnemonic that eventually evolved into 'Hell Hole,' and from that title came the whole idea. We all contributed lyrics. That was one of the songs that we all wrote together."

A note for the keen-eared: near the end of the performance of this song in the film, you can hear someone yell, "Do 'Stonehenge'!" Nobody actually yelled this while we were shooting. We added it in postproduction to foreshadow the return of an old number that Tap had scrapped from its live show. In the sequel, we also added a "Do 'Stonehenge'!" shout from an audience member in postproduction. But this time, it comes while the band is already playing "Stonehenge." We justified this misguided shout as the product of a concertgoer's abuse of drugs, stupidity, or, most likely, a combination of both.

*The window's dirty*
*The mattress stinks*
*This ain't no place to be a man*

# JUST WANT TO MAKE SOME EARDRUMS BLEED

*Ain't got no future*
*Ain't got no past*
*And I don't think I ever can*

*The floor is filthy*
*The walls are thin*
*The wind is howling in my face*

*The rats are peeling*
*I'm losing ground*
*Can't seem to join the human race*

*I'm living in a*
*Hell hole*
*Don't want to stay in this*
*Hell hole*
*Don't want to die in this*
*Hell hole*
*Girl, get me out of this*
*Hell hole*

*I rode the jet stream*
*I hit the top*
*I'm eating steak and lobster tails*

*The sauna's drafty*
*The pool's too hot*
*The kitchen stinks of boiling snails*

*The taxman's coming*
*The butler quit*
*This ain't no place to be a man*

*I'm going back*
*To where I started*
*I'm flashing back into my pan*

*It's better in a*
*Hell hole*
*You know where you stand in a*
*Hell hole*
*Folks lend a hand in a*
*Hell hole*
*Girl, get me back to my*
*Hell hole*

## "Sex Farm"

Another song that began with a Chris Guest lick. As with "Hell Hole," we all chipped in on the lyrics. And as with "Big Bottom," the double entendres just flew out of us: "Scratching in your henhouse." "Hosing down your barn door." "Crouching in your pea patch."

Recalls Michael, "It was originally called 'Bone Farm,' but we changed it because of a metaphor issue. 'Bone Farm' sounds like it's referring to a graveyard. So we thought, 'Let's just come right out and be flagrantly obvious about it.'"

# JUST WANT TO MAKE SOME EARDRUMS BLEED

*Working on a sex farm*
*Trying to raise some hard love*
*Getting out my pitchfork*
*Poking your hay*

*Scratching in your henhouse*
*Sniffing at your feedbag*
*Slipping out your back door*
*Leaving my spray*

*Sex farm woman*
*I'm gonna mow you down*
*Sex farm woman*
*I'll rake and hoe you down*
*Sex farm woman*
*Don't you see my silo risin' high, high, high, high*

*Working on a sex farm*
*Hosing down your barn door*
*Bothering your livestock*
*They know what I need*

*Working up a hot sweat*
*Crouching in your pea patch*
*Plowing through your bean field*
*Planting my seed*

*Sex farm woman*
*I'll be your hired hand*

*Sex farm woman*
*I'll let my offer stand*
*Sex farm woman*
*Don't you hear my tractor rumbling by, by, by, by*

*Working on a sex farm*
*Trying to raise some hard love*
*Getting out my pitchfork*
*Poking your hay!*

## "Stonehenge"

This song showcases the movie's biggest (or smallest, depending on how you look at it) visual gag. It was written by Michael and Chris at a house Chris had rented in Studio City. It started out with the two of them noodling on acoustic guitars. "We pretty much wrote it all in one day," says Michael, "really pushing the idea of peak pretension: 'Stonehenge! / Where a man's a man / And the children dance to the pipes of Pan.' It was essential in our minds, for the pomposity of it all, to begin with a spoken-word part, a recitative. So that's how we got Chris saying, 'In ancient times / hundreds of years before the dawn of history / lived a strange race of people, the Druids.'

"We did that, and then my verses, and then Chris's bridge part: 'And you, my love . . .' We had everything but an ending. We thought about writing a third verse, but we never got around to it, because in the movie, the scene cuts during the part where Chris is playing mandolin and the dwarves are dancing around the miniature Stonehenge replica."

"I wrote the mandolin melody," Chris recalls. "It is, in style, reminiscent of various Irish fiddle tunes. I began playing mandolin in high school and played a lot of bluegrass, which has its roots in the same music.

"We had this song for the demo reel. I played the mandolin melody for John Sinclair, our keyboardist then, and he started playing along in real time, doing the thirds right away. He gave it this pipe sound that we have copied ever since."

"When we recorded the song for the soundtrack album," adds Michael, "we realized we needed to figure out an ending. So we wrote a sequel to the opening recitative: 'And where are they now / The little people of Stonehenge? / And what would they say to us / If we were here, tonight?'

"That doesn't even make sense. We just wrote it to make each other laugh. There's a line in a later Tap song, 'The Majesty of Rock,' where David sings, 'I know, for I told me so.' It's like, is he making a mistake or is that exactly what he means? 'If we were here tonight'— does that mean that we are not really here? Anyway, it made us laugh."

*In ancient times,*
*Hundreds of years before the dawn of history*
*Lived a strange race of people, the Druids*

*No one knows who they were or what they were doing*
*But their legacy remains*
*Hewn into the living rock, of Stonehenge*

*Stonehenge!*
*Where the demons dwell*
*Where the banshees live and they do live well*
*Stonehenge!*

*Where a man's a man*
*And the children dance to the pipes of Pan*

*Stonehenge!*
*'Tis a magic place*
*Where the moon doth rise with a dragon's face*
*Stonehenge!*
*Where the virgins lie*
*And the prayers of devils fill the midnight sky*

*And you, my love, won't you take my hand*
*We'll go back in time to that mystic land*
*Where the dewdrops cry and the cats meow*
*I will take you there*
*I will show you how*

*And oh, how they danced*
*The little children of Stonehenge*
*Beneath the haunted moon*
*For fear that daybreak might come too soon*

*[Mandolin break, dancing Druids, lowering of tiny Stonehenge]*

*And where are they now?*
*The little people of Stonehenge*
*And what would they say to us?*
*If we were here, tonight*

## "Rock 'n' Roll Creation"

In Tap lore, "Rock 'n' Roll Creation" is Spinal Tap's cosmic take on the origin of the universe. It's also the keynote song of a concept album whose unfavorable review Marty reads aloud to the band: "This pretentious, ponderous collection of religious rock psalms is enough to prompt the question 'What day did the Lord create Spinal Tap, and couldn't He have rested on that day, too?'" And it's another song ripe for a sight gag. It provided the opportunity for a band member—Derek, specifically—to get stuck inside a cocoon-like pod for the entire length of the performance.

Says Chris, "That song is really fun to play because it has those big chords. Then I do some guitar noodling, and then there's that harmony section where we sing, 'I look to the stars and the answer is clear / I look in the mirror and see what I fear.'

"It's the same idea as 'Stonehenge': they're going for *profound*. 'Ying was searching for his yang / And he looked and he saw that it was good.' They think that they've arrived at something deep there. If you read interviews with real bands, you'll often find them describing their writing process in a self-serious way: 'When we wrote that song, we finally knew that we were serious songwriters.' That's how David and Nigel felt. It's a profound song about absolutely nothing."

*When there was darkness*
*And the void was king and ruled the elements,*
*When there was silence*
*And the hush was almost deafening!*

*Out of the emptiness*
*(Salvation!) Salvation!*
*Rhythm and light and sound*

*'Twas the rock 'n' roll creation*
*'Twas a terrible big bang*
*'Twas the ultimate mutation*
*Ying was searching for his yang*
*And he looked and he saw that it was good!*

*When I'm alone beneath the stars and feeling insignificant*
*I turn within to see the forces that created me*

*I look to the stars and the answer is clear*
*I look in the mirror and see what I fear*

*'Tis the rock 'n' roll creation*
*'Tis the absolute rebirth*
*'Tis the rolling of the ocean and the rocking of the earth*
*And I looked and I saw that it was good!*

**In** creating these songs, we never wanted the humor to come from the music. It would always be in the lyrics. Harry explains, "The words that we used in lyrics and titles, that had to be the funny part. But we all agreed that we weren't going to do bad music. There's nothing funny about that unless you're Spike Jones. Also, we wanted the songs to be fun to play, and it's not fun to play bad music. So the music was a carrier of the humor rather than a source of the humor."

We had no idea when we were coming up with these songs, just trying to make each other laugh, that they would have any kind of staying power, to the point that people who first saw the movie forty years ago still remember and sing them. But we all knew that these were quality songs. It's been said by more than one critic that for such a maligned and humiliated band, Spinal Tap's tunes are actually pretty catchy.

CHAPTER 7

# Tonight I'm Gonna Rock You

We had the songs. We had the treatment. We had the financing. We had five weeks scheduled for shooting.

There was still one element missing before we could begin. I didn't love Marty DiBergi's look in the demo reel. Whenever you look at production photos from movie sets, you invariably see the director wearing a baseball cap. In the demo reel, Marty wore a cowboy hat. Wasn't right. Had to be a baseball cap. And I thought, "To project strength and authority, go military."

I found a perfect cap. It was black with yellow embroidery on the brim that the military refers to as "scrambled eggs." The words USS CORAL SEA, the name of a U.S. Navy aircraft carrier, were stitched in gold above the visor. But to my disappointment, Karen Murphy informed me that de Forest Research, the clearances company we were working with, couldn't get permission from the U.S. military for me to wear the hat. We were not allowed to use the name of the actual Navy vessel.

So, crafty producer that she was, Karen came up with a solution. She got out a needle and thread and personally altered the *C* in *Coral* to make it an *O*. Now Marty's hat read USS OORAL SEA.

With that, both Marty and I were ready to direct our first movie.

On Monday, November 8, 1982, the cast and crew gathered at Carthay Studios on West Pico Boulevard to shoot the first scene of *This Is Spinal Tap*. We re-created a 1967 TV show, *Jamboreebop*, that presented Spinal Tap in full psychedelic regalia as they performed their only single to make the U.S. charts, "(Listen to the) Flower People."

Chris, Michael, and Harry were joined by Russ Kunkel, the original Spinal Tap drummer from *The TV Show*, again wearing his Afro wig. Russ had now been dubbed Eric "Stumpy Joe" Childs, the drummer who, we would learn in an interview sequence filmed the following day, had died by choking on vomit. More on that in a moment.

I had spent time in Haight-Ashbury in 1967 and had vivid memories of it. Among them: making love on Owsley acid, seeing Janis Joplin with Big Brother and the Holding Company at the Fillmore, and having the distinction of overhearing Janis having sex with a friend of mine in his apartment overlooking Ghirardelli Square. It truly was the Summer of Love. And having worked on *The Smothers Brothers Show* and having seen tons of rock acts on television, I knew exactly what our sixties-style TV psychedelic number should look like. We had a Milton Glaser–type pop-art set. In a setup for the song that we later cut, the band is introduced by a semi-hip host in a mustard-colored turtleneck, played by an actor named Richard Marion. "They're from England and don't let the name scare you—they're full of love," he says. "Please welcome Spinal Tap."

In keeping with the Summer of Love vibe, the grinning, insouciant David St. Hubbins of the "Gimme Some Money" clip was replaced by a solemn hippie sage in an embroidered vest. Nigel Tufnel's pageboy haircut appeared for the first time. Derek Smalls already had his handlebar mustache, but his hair was shorter and his look considerably less edgy than it would become in Tap's metal years. During Nigel's solo, in fact, Derek looks into the camera and mouths the words "We love you" to the folks in TV land.

"I did it simply because it was so powerfully stupid," says Harry. "We were mining the power of stupidity. I can't recall definitively, but I believe it just spontaneously appeared and we kept it in."

On that same day, we shot a Beatles-style press conference in which the stoned sixties iteration of Tap parried questions from American reporters.

**REPORTER:** How do you find the women in America?

**DAVID:** Turn left at the men.

This scene would be the first of many to end up on the proverbial cutting-room floor. We may have been inexperienced as filmmakers, but we were never at a loss for ideas. I shot three hours of interview footage alone, which meant there would be a lot of work separating the wheat from the chaff.

Having Marty DiBergi on-screen as the band's interviewer was an unorthodox choice for a documentary. You don't often physically see the filmmaker. But in an homage to Marty Scorsese's on-camera presence in *The Last Waltz*, we decided to give our Marty his time in the sun. And if I'm being honest, I knew it wouldn't hurt if the first face the audience saw was the guy they knew from *All in the Family*.

Like Alistair Cooke on *Masterpiece Theatre*, Marty welcomes the viewer to *This Is Spinal Tap*. Wearing his Brian De Palma safari jacket, the USS OORAL SEA military cap, and a viewfinder around his neck that you never see him actually use, he looks straight into the camera and delivers the cold opening to the film:

> . . . So in the late fall of 1982, when I heard that Tap was releasing a new album called *Smell the Glove* and was planning their first tour of the United States in almost six years to promote that album, well, needless to say, I jumped at the chance to make the documentary—the, if you will, rockumentary—that you're about to see. I wanted to capture the sights, the sounds, the *smells*, of a hardworking rock band on the road. And I got that. But I got more. A lot more.
>
> But hey, enough of my yakkin'. Whaddya say? Let's boogie!

More importantly, Marty presides over the interview sequence interspersed in bits and pieces between action scenes throughout the film. Shot in front of a baronial estate on our second day of shooting, this sequence yielded the scene in which Marty reads aloud to Tap some negative reviews of their albums (Marty: "The review you had on *Shark Sandwich* was merely a two-word review: 'Shit sandwich.'" Derek: "You cahn't print that!") and the scene in which David, Nigel, and Derek tell Marty the stories of how their drummers died.

The guys never knew what I was going to throw at them. While I wrote the negative reviews of their albums in advance, they always came up with spontaneous responses that were brilliant. By the same token, while I was aware that Tap had a tragic track record with drummers, I didn't know exactly how each drummer died until I asked about them. We surprised each other, which made the interview sequences more organic.

But sometimes it was tough holding it together and we'd break. There are instances when you can be too fuckin' organic.

The riff on the death of Tap's second drummer, Eric "Stumpy Joe" Childs, was a master class in improv teamwork, with Harry, Chris, and Michael fluidly executing their interplay like Tinker, Evers, and Chance. (Another shameless baseball reference à la Al Gionfriddo, this time to three old-time Chicago Cubs infielders who were proficient at turning double plays.) The underlying premise was that Stumpy Joe had choked on vomit—a sad trope in the annals of premature rock deaths, from Jimi Hendrix to John Bonham.

"We knew that it was going to involve choking on vomit," says Michael, "but we also knew that Harry couldn't say Stumpy Joe 'choked on his own vomit,' which is what a coroner's report would say. Basically, we knew where it was going to go, but not *how* it was going to go."

Here's how it actually went:

**DEREK:** It's not a very pleasant story . . . The official explanation was, he choked on vomit.

**NIGEL:** It was actually someone else's vomit.

**DEREK:** They can't prove whose vomit it was.

**DAVID:** Well, there's no prints. There's no way of inspecting and photographing.

**NIGEL:** You can't really dust for vomit.

This sequence was shot in Beachwood Canyon, five miles due west of the Hollywood sign, on the grounds of a gaudy faux castle built sometime in the 1970s. "The cheesiest thing you've ever seen," Chris recalls. "It was sad that some person had built that to show 'Look at how much money I have.' But there *was* an emu on the property. That was the most interesting thing about it."

This edifice has since acquired an official name, the Hollywood Castle, and has racked up an impressive CV as the location for Katy Perry's "I Kissed a Girl" video and a variety of soft-core porn films.

We never explicitly stated whose baronial home this was meant to be, though our bible contained a reference to "Nigel's castle in Lichtenstein" and our longer treatment placed the castle in Scotland. Chris decided to wear a kilt in proper lord-of-the-manor style.

Michael, as the band's threadhead, wore a smart umber blazer with white trousers. David was the most tastefully dressed member of Tap, favoring tailored jackets and early-eighties skinny ties.

"Our costume person, Renee Johnston, took us to a little shop on Melrose Avenue that had just started called Let It Rock," recalls Michael. "This was before Melrose had really exploded as a shopping district. The store was somehow affiliated with Vivienne Westwood and Malcolm McLaren in London."

Harry had his own twist on the gentleman-squire look, having Derek puff on a Sherlock Holmes–style calabash pipe while wearing a brown leather jacket over a Shrewsbury Town F.C. shirt. "I'd been in London and I'd come across a street-corner stand selling football jerseys," Harry says. "I saw the Shrewsbury one and thought, 'Well, that's a team that is never going to be in the lead in the Premier League.' So I thought it was the appropriate jersey to get."

Onstage, Derek chose a more racy look popularized by Rob Halford, the lead singer of Judas Priest. He wore a bondage harness over his bare skin. "Renee refused to shop for my harness," Harry says. "She sent me to the Pleasure Chest on Santa Monica Boulevard in West Hollywood. Chris and Karen Murphy went with me. I had the experience of walking into the Pleasure Chest and asking, 'Where are the harnesses?' The answer was 'Between the butt plugs and the ball stretchers.'"

Chris, too, has vivid recall of this errand. "I had never been and haven't been since," he says. "It was an unfamiliar world, eye-opening and . . . other-orifice-opening. We were wandering through these aisles and seeing things we'd never seen. There were molded arms a yard long with fists at the end of them."

Strange as it was, the shopping trip proved a rousing success. "I found the harnesses where they were supposed to be, between the butt plugs and the ball stretchers," says Harry. "I also saw, displayed on a shelf in jars, these things labeled 'Doc Johnson's Butt Plugs.' Years later, my wife and I were at an auto show looking at a rare original Corvette in mint condition. As in most museums, there was a credit for whose collection this came from. And the credit read 'From the Doc Johnson Collection.'"

The same Doc Johnson? One can only hope.

The contrast between the staid clothes Derek wore offstage and the provocative clothes he wore onstage was by design. "It seemed to me, in observing heavy metal bands, that the most out-there representative of the band in terms of garb was contradictorily the least like that in real life," Harry says. "Bass players are almost always less flamboyant as human beings than guitarists."

For the film to have the right look and feel, I needed a cameraman who had experience shooting rock documentaries. Peter Smokler had a long history of shooting concert films and rock docs, having begun his career as a camera operator on the Maysles brothers' notorious Rolling Stones documentary, *Gimme Shelter*. Peter had the unfortunate distinction of being at the Altamont Speedway when a fan was killed by a Hells Angel. At the beginning of our shoot, Peter couldn't quite grasp what we were doing. At one point he said to me, "I don't get what's funny about this. It's not any different from what bands do in the documentaries I've worked on."

I told him that we were playing things close to the bone, just tilting them a bit. He got it. The truth is, we were flying by the seat of our pants. In a first pass at a scene, I'd tell Peter to keep his handheld Arriflex 16mm camera trained on whoever was talking. But once we shot two or three takes, I realized that to cut together the funniest stuff from each take, we needed to have reaction shots to cut away to. So I'd have Peter do a take where he'd just focus on people listening.

There were times when I stood behind Peter and whispered in his ear telling him where to go. Sometimes I even physically, like a dolly grip, moved his body into position. Peter quickly came to have an innate feel for the flow of a scene and had great instincts for being at the right place at the right time—as he was when he caught Ian Faith's look of utter bafflement when Bobbi Flekman says, "Money talks and bullshit walks."

We never shot a scene more than four times. After that, the spontaneity and the realness would dissipate. Though it must be said that in Chris's case, repetitiveness was never an issue: he was always so in the moment that he rarely remembered what he had said in a previous take. It might not match anything that preceded it, but it was never stale and always funny.

For the concert sequences, we used three cameras and shot each song three times, giving me nine angles to cut with. Critically, we always made sure to get the classic heavy-rock crotch shot, shooting from below and focusing on a band member's member. I don't want to be accused of self-horn-tooting, but I feel we were pioneers of this cinematic technique. Just check out any Mötley Crüe or Poison video from the 1980s.

Because we were operating on such a low budget, we had to shoot the concert scenes, which ostensibly took place in cities all over the country, entirely in Los Angeles. In one eighteen-hour day, just like a band on tour, with the crew loading and unloading equipment, we actually went to five different auditoriums.

For "Tonight I'm Gonna Rock You Tonight," Tap's first song in the film, we splurged, rounding up about six hundred extras. We wanted to show Tap playing before a big crowd. But for the remainder of the shoot, we had to make do with only forty to sixty extras for each concert scene. Taking a page from the Roger Corman school of micro-budget filmmaking, we strategically moved the extras around from one shot to the next to create the illusion of a crowd. To give the impression of a packed house, we'd put a handful of extras directly in front of the camera and then cram the rest in front of the stage, so no one would notice that the auditorium was nearly empty.

For "Jazz Odyssey," which we shot at the Magic Mountain theme park in Valencia, there was no need to fake a big crowd. With Tap reduced to second billing behind a puppet show, the sparse daytime crowd was perfect.

Even though *This Is Spinal Tap* was my first film, I didn't feel nervous about it. Everything just felt right. We were all experienced improvisers—not just as actors but as a production team, making adjustments on the fly.

Consider, for example, the scene in which Tap is about to check into a hotel when they're diverted by the arrival of a more popular rock star, Duke Fame ("of Duke Fame and the Fame-Throwers," per our treatment). The musician we cast to play Duke, Paul Shortino, looked perfect for the part but wasn't blessed with the schnadle gene. So at the last minute, I asked Howard Hesseman, my Committee castmate—who at the time was starring as Dr. Johnny Fever in the TV series *WKRP in Cincinnati*—to play Duke's arrogant manager, Terry Ladd. This was a character who had not existed twenty-four hours earlier. Howard jumped right in.

He slicked back his hair, put on a camouflage jumpsuit, turned up the collar of his leather jacket, and delivered a perfect performance, controlling the scene so Duke Fame could just stand there and look perfect. Terry dismissively calls Ian Faith "Liam." And when David asks him where Duke is playing, Terry nonchalantly says, "We're doing the, uh, EnormoDome, whatever it is, it's terrific." When Ian attempts to engage Terry as an equal, Howard delivers one of the best lines in the film: "Listen, we'd love to stand around and chat, but we gotta sit down in the lobby and wait for the limo"—the perfect brush-off.

Paul Benedict had already played the hotel's check-in clerk in the demo reel. But the second time around, he showed up with a couple of surprises: a wavy-hair wig and thick Coke-bottle glasses that made him look twenty years older than he was. When Ian belittles the clerk as a "twisted old fruit," Paul's character indignantly replies, "I'm just as God made me, sir."

We didn't break character often, but with Paul, we struggled to keep it together. Recalls Michael, "At one point, Hendra put his cricket bat up on the counter and Paul said, 'Well, you can't take that to your room.' Tony said, 'Why not?' and Paul said, 'Well, it's *enormous*.' He was into the second syllable of *enormous* and we were already gone."

Another moment of beauty that didn't make it into the film.

**F**red Willard also got to us. He chose to play the U.S. Air Force's Bob Hookstratten not as a militaristic hard-ass, but as a genial, accommodating lieutenant. Fred has only about ninety seconds of screen time, but it's ninety seconds of gold.

"With Fred it was always, 'You're in good hands, but strap in,'" says Michael. "Martin Mull, who worked with him on the show *Fernwood 2 Night*, liked to say, 'The thing you've got to remember about Fred is that he doesn't use his turn signal.'"

Fred nailed Chris as he led the confused band around the military base:

> **LIEUTENANT HOOKSTRATTEN:** Let me explain a bit about what's going on. This is our monthly "At Ease Weekend." It gives us a chance to kind of let down our hair, although I see you all have a head start. These haircuts wouldn't pass military muster, believe me. Although I shouldn't talk, my hair's get-

ting a little shaggy, too. If I get too close to you, they'll think I'm part of the band.

I'm joking, of course. Shall we go in?

"If you watch that scene, when Fred says, 'I shouldn't talk,' I'm hiding out from the law," Chris says. "I'm ducking behind David Kaffinetti because I couldn't hold it any longer. It was just *boom*—I went down."

**W**henever a guest performer like Howard or Paul or Fred came on the set, it was like a jolt of adrenaline. The hotel scene yielded my favorite line in the film, the one that gives this book its title. After Duke Fame walks away, David and Nigel raise the subject of Duke's latest album cover, in which he is tied down to a table while nude women stand over him with whips. David appeals to Ian: "The point is, it's much worse than *Smell the Glove*."

Ian points out that the difference is that on Fame's cover, *he* is the submissive one, whereas on the sexist *Smell the Glove* cover, the female model being forced to smell the glove is the victim. To the band, the light bulb turns on.

"See, he did a little twist on it!" says Nigel.

David then chimes in, "It's such a fine line between stupid and—"

"—and clever," Derek says.

I loved everything about this moment: the inadvertent profundity of the statement and the seamless Chris-to-Michael-to-Harry handoff. (There it is, baseball fans: Tinker to Evers to Chance.) You'll notice that Harry is off-camera when he says, "And clever." We didn't have coverage of him. But it didn't matter. It worked.

We had to shoot Paul Shaffer's scenes over a single weekend because he was busy being Dave Letterman's bandleader during the week. Lindsay Doran, the executive in charge of production, ran interference between the folks at Embassy and me. They thought it was wasteful to fly Paul in, because there was a chance of a snowstorm in New York that weekend that might cause him to miss his flight.

Lindsay told me that, as a cost-saving measure, the studio recommended I cut Artie Fufkin from the movie. I resisted and went into production improv mode: "No. If Paul makes it, great. And if he somehow gets snowed in, we'll make the scene be about *that*— that the band's PR gets fucked up because the rep from Polymer Records was snowed in."

Fortunately, Paul made his flight and we were able to capture Artie Fufkin in all his glorious ineptitude. In our treatment, we made repeated references to Artie as "coked-up." But Paul brought such a sweet desperation to his character that the idea of any drug influence seemed wrong. Another moment of beauty that didn't make the cut happens before the band's disastrous zero-attendance record store appearance, the one that prompts Artie's famous "Kick my ass" plea. We shot a scene where the members of Tap are hanging out with a bunch of groupies in a hotel room while Artie begs them to make an appearance on a local radio station at the rock-star-unfriendly hour of 7 a.m. When they complain about having to get up so early, Artie, in his desperation, resorts to doing something that Paul remembered having done before.

"In the seventies, when I was trying to do the show with Norman Lear about a rock band, I was mad that it was getting nowhere," Paul says. "I vented my feelings one day to Chris and Tom Leopold.

I picked up an egg and smashed it on my head in frustration. Chris never forgot it."

So in the "Cutting Room Floor" section of the Criterion Collection DVD edition of *This Is Spinal Tap*, you can find Artie/Paul losing his mind over the band's resistance. He says, "What do I gotta do to get you to a radio station at seven in the morning? It's not such a big deal! Do I have to take my whole family and chain 'em to a radio station to get a record played?" He then picks up a soft-boiled egg from a room-service cart, smashes it on his forehead, and says, "Do I have to take a thing with an egg and smash the thing in my face to get a record played on the air?"

That was a tough one to cut. But sometimes you have to kill your darlings. I felt this scene bled too much into the "Kick my ass" scene.

Comedy is not generally about smart," says Chris. "You don't see Laurel and Hardy come in to do a job and execute it perfectly. The basis of a lot of our comedy in Spinal Tap is that they have some kind of pretense that they're smart, but they're a little thick."

This was evident in the scene where Nigel shows Marty DiBergi his guitar collection and the custom amps that the Marshall company had made for Tap. You'll remember that in Marty's opening, he talks about Spinal Tap being "England's loudest band." But how do you prove this assertion? How do you show it visually?

Chris came up with the idea of having our prop people create a metal plate that could be overlaid on a real Marshall amp, thereby allowing Nigel to crank the dials past ten, to eleven. This prompted the following exchange:

MARTY: Does that mean it's louder? Is it any louder?

NIGEL: Well, it's one louder, isn't it? It's not ten. You see, most blokes, they'll be playing at ten—you're on ten, all the way up, you're on ten on your guitar, where can you go from there? Where?

MARTY: I don't know.

NIGEL: Nowhere, exactly! What we do is, if we need that extra push over the cliff, you know what we do?

MARTY: Put it up to eleven.

NIGEL: Eleven, exactly! One louder.

When we shot this scene, neither Chris nor I knew that I was going to challenge Nigel's logic. But with Chris being the brilliant improviser that he is, I knew that backing him into a corner was like throwing him a 75-mph fastball over the heart of the plate; it would wind up in the second deck. (Again with the baseball.) It was the same with Mel Brooks and my dad when they did the *2000 Year Old Man* albums. Whenever my dad had Mel boxed in, with seemingly no escape, that's when Mel would come up with his funniest stuff.

So Marty says to Nigel, "Why don't you just make ten louder and make ten be the top number, and make *that* a little louder?"

And there it was, the 75-mph fastball.

Chris, a huge wad of gum in his mouth, stared at me for a long beat, waiting for the pitch to reach the plate. Then he swung and went yard.

He said blankly, "These go to eleven."

At the time, we had no idea that Chris's simple response would enter the zeitgeist, become iconic, and eventually make it into the lexicon via *The Oxford English Dictionary*.

**L**ooking back, I'm forever grateful for Lindsay Doran. She allowed us to work unfettered, keeping Embassy's concerns at bay.

I have only recently learned about some of the things she spared us from. For instance, in the scene where Nigel complains to Ian about the backstage catering provisions—the Van Halen–inspired moment—we see the band, ready to go onstage, decked out in their concert gear and makeup. Nigel has glitter on his eyelids as he voices his displeasure to Ian. "This miniature bread—I've been working with this for about half an hour," he says. Ian suggests to Nigel that he simply fold the cold cuts into a size befitting the tiny bread. This flies right past Nigel's comprehension. Then he goes on to point out the inconsistency of the pitted green olives—some have pimentos inside and others don't: "Look, look, who's in here? No one. And then in here, there's a little guy, look! So it's a complete catastrophe."

"One day, somebody at Embassy said, 'I want to see some dailies,'" Lindsay says. "I thought the funniest thing I had seen at that point was the scene where Chris is going through all the food. So I showed it to the executive—just the two of us in a screening room. He didn't laugh once. At the end of it, the lights came up, and all he said was 'Do they have to wear all that eye makeup?' That was his note. I began to worry. I thought, 'What's going to happen? They're never going to understand this movie.'"

CHAPTER 8

# And I Looked and I Saw That It Was Good

With Lindsay shielding us from the powers that be, we blindly and happily pressed forward. We were having fun, and, I thought, coming up with some good stuff. We had this idea that while the band was hanging out in their hotel in Memphis, they would hear one of their songs pop up on an oldies station. As the song ends, the slick AM deejay, voiced by Harry, says, "Going *allll* the way back to 1965, that one. Doesn't it feel good? With the Thamesmen and 'Cups and Cakes.' Of course, the Thamesmen later changed their name to Spinal Tap."

This gets the guys all excited, until the deejay adds that Tap is "currently residing in the 'Where Are They Now?' file." In a perfect moment of wordless acting, Michael's face goes from sheer delight to utter depression.

In one cut of the film, we had a scene between "Cups and Cakes" and David, Nigel, and Derek's visit to Elvis Presley's grave at Graceland. In that scene, Ian tries to buck the guys up after the deejay's diss and urges them to get their frustrations out by trashing the hotel room. Wielding his cricket bat, he proceeds to lay waste to the furniture, the food on the room-service table, and the TV set.

The remnants of that scene appear in a flurry of quick cuts to Ian's cricket-bat destruction during an interview with Marty in which Ian describes the bat as "a kind of totemistic thing. To be quite frank with you, it's come in useful in a couple of situations. Certainly in the topsy-turvy world of heavy rock, having a good, solid piece of wood in your hand is quite often useful."

We shot that interview in the office of an L.A. recording studio called the Record Plant, the same location where Ian tries to convince Marty that Tap isn't losing popularity—rather, "their appeal is becoming more selective." Tony Hendra wasn't always the easiest guy to work with—he could be, as Chris says, "a bit of a scoundrel"—but he invariably came up with the perfect quip.

Given that *This Is Spinal Tap* was shot entirely in the L.A. area, we had to get creative about the visit to Graceland. We wound up using a patch of park in Altadena, which we decorated with wreaths, rosettes, and flower arrangements. I have to say, it looked pretty authentic. We did, however, mess up one thing: on Elvis's gravestone, his middle name is spelled wrong. We had it as "Aaron," with two *a*'s. His parents, Vernon and Gladys Presley, spelled it with only one *a*.

We were limited as to which Elvis song Tap could serenade the King with as they stood before his grave. The rights to our original choice, "Love Me Tender," were held by Presley's estate: a nonstarter. The big Leiber and Stoller hits—"Hound Dog," "Jailhouse Rock"—were also way out of our price range. Fortunately, we were allowed to use Elvis's first major hit, "Heartbreak Hotel." It happened that one of its cowriters was Mae Boren Axton, the mother of singer-songwriter Hoyt Axton. She was still alive and kind enough to grant us the rights.

I'm not sure if we ever cleared the rights for the Frank Sinatra standard "All the Way." Probably not, because we cut the scene it was used in. After Tommy (Bruno Kirby), the Sinatra-loving limo driver, innocently delivers pizzas to the band, he is coaxed by Nigel and Derek into taking a few hits from a joint. This results in Tommy losing his inhibitions . . . and his clothes.

Stripped down to nothing but his black bikini briefs and black socks held up by garters, Tommy delivers an impassioned performance of "All the Way" into a pizza crust he uses as a microphone. After he belts out the last notes—"It's for sure I'm gonna love you alll . . . thhhe . . . waaaaay"—Tommy looks at the band, says, "*That's* music," and proceeds to pass out.

As great as Bruno was, the scene didn't advance the story. And so another darling bit the dust.

Throughout the filmmaking process, we were faced with a number of tough decisions. Derek's trouser-stuffing humiliation at the hands of airport security originally had a long and incredibly involved antecedent. On Tap's tour bus, we had Derek showing Marty a scene from an Italian gangster movie he had played a small part in, Marco Zamboni's *Roma '79*. Decked out in a white suit and matching fedora, Derek assembles a shotgun and points it out his window. But before he can get a shot off, he becomes the victim, taking a bullet in his back.

While Marty and Derek are absorbed watching *Roma '79*, David and Nigel confer in the background, then summon Derek for a private chat.

"We'd like a word with you about your stage . . . appearance," David says. "Specifically the costuming during performance. It may be something might be missing in terms of, uh—"

"Thrust," says Nigel helpfully, adding, "There's sort of a canyon where there should be a mountain."

Thus, Derek's trouser-stuffing is born. In the demo reel, when he sets off the airport metal detector, he removes a bandanna full of nuts and bolts from his pants.

But by the time we got to the film, we decided that Derek's bulge should be some kind of phallic vegetable wrapped in aluminum foil, akin to whatever torpedo-like object Chris had seen sliding down the pant leg of the British rocker he'd encountered in Matt Umanov's guitar shop. The foil aspect of the story, says Michael, was an allusion to a Hollywood rumor that a famous director had been busted for trying to smuggle cocaine through a security check by wrapping it, idiotically, in foil.

In an additional scene we shot but also didn't use, Derek is seen during a sound check with the band's roadie, Moke, discussing which penile produce item would work best for bulge enhancement. (This idea did make its way onto the Grimsby card that read MOKE MAKES DEREK DICKS.)

But in the end, we wondered if all of this was necessary for the metal-detector gag to pay off. The reveal, we decided, worked better without the prolonged setup.

However, we must not gloss over the chosen object that causes Derek's humiliation. Over the years, Harry has felt the need to make clear that the item he stuffed down his trousers was *not* a cucumber. "A cucumber is too large and warty to achieve the desired effect," he says. It was, he insists, a courgette—otherwise known as a zucchini.

How passionate is Harry on this topic? Suffice it to say that the name of his record label is Courgette Records. He is equally hell-bent on explaining why the courgette was wrapped in foil. "The idea of it setting off the metal detector was secondary," he says. "First of all, we concluded that the courgette was the proper implement to achieve the desired goal. As for the foil, look: if you've got an unwrapped courgette between a tight pant leg and your actual leg, and you're onstage sweating, you're going to have a fucking mess on your hands—actually, on your legs—within twenty minutes. The foil was to prevent the liquefaction of the courgette."

Aren't you glad we cleared that up?

By the way, if you listen closely to the audio in this scene, you can hear Harry's and Chris's voices doing the airport PA announcements: "Midwest Airlines, Flight 406 . . . Grand Forks, scheduled for departure at Gate 12, has been delayed approximately twenty minutes . . ." Nowadays, these voice-over cameos would be called Easter eggs, little nuggets for observant fans to have fun discovering. But in 1982, this was called "We don't have enough money to pay anyone else."

The band's roadie, Moke, was played by a great guy named Robert Bauer. If you watch the movie all the way through, you'll notice that in the end credits, he is listed as "And Robert Bauer as Moke ." Why was the character's name in a box? Isn't it obvious? No, you say? Okay, I'll explain. We had all just seen a movie called *Butterfly*, a vanity project financed by the Israeli businessman Meshulam Riklis that starred his much younger wife, Pia Zadora. In the film, the actor James Franciscus was listed as "Moke Blue." To give more prominence to Franciscus, who in the 1960s had starred in his own TV series, *Mr. Novak*, they encased his name in a box. We didn't necessarily think that Robert Bauer had achieved the requisite status to have his name in a box. But that didn't mean his character's name didn't deserve one. Hence, Moke in a box. Certainly, you can see why it was imperative that we do that.

Moke's big moment comes during the performance of "Rock 'n' Roll Creation," when Derek gets trapped inside his pod. In reality, the pods weren't automated. Crew members crouched below them, manually opening them slowly so that the band members could dramatically emerge. As the stuck Derek becomes more frustrated, Moke runs onstage and frantically attempts to free him. First he checks the pod's circuitry. Then he tries prying it open with his hands. When that doesn't work, he pounds on it with a hammer. No luck. Finally he attacks it with a blowtorch. Somehow this works and Derek springs free, only to realize that the song is ending and his bandmates are returning to their pods. In a final indignity, Derek rushes to get back into his pod, only to have it close on him. With him half in and half out, he raises his fist in a triumphant gesture, as if this was what he meant to do all along.

We debated the hammering. The guys in the band argued that given the high decibel level of their instruments, Moke's hammering would not have been audible to the audience. Technically, of course, they were right. But hey, when a laugh is at stake, logic has to take a back seat. Sometimes, you just gotta say "Fuck it" and drop your pants. In the end, we cranked up the clunking of Moke's hammer. And the laugh was preserved.

**E**xactly what is an Australian's nightmare? Tony Hendra is no longer with us, so we'll never know for sure. But his explosive reaction to David's suggestion that Jeanine join the tour as Tap's comanager was Ian's finest hour. Turning to Jeanine, who was wearing a lamé blazer, raspberry-colored leggings, a scarf wrapped around her head, and about ten pounds of costume jewelry, he said, "Look, this is my position, okay? I am not managing [the band] with you or any other woman. Especially one that dresses like an Australian's nightmare. So fuck you and fuck all of you, because *I quit!*"

June Chadwick recalls, "A lot of Jeanine's clothes were my clothes. I had great fun with the wardrobe lady, Renee Johnston, going through my things and saying, 'Let's put that with that.' And then the makeup gal put way too much eye makeup on, and the whole thing looked . . . nightmarish."

This scene comes in the immediate aftermath of the "Stonehenge" debacle, which is a result of Nigel's suggestion that they rescue their faltering tour by reviving "Stonehenge" because it offers "the best production value we've ever had onstage." Nigel, however, makes a crucial error. On a napkin, he writes down that the monolith's dimensions are eighteen inches by eighteen inches rather than eighteen feet. When the set designer, played by Anjelica Huston, delivers the prop as requested, it's so small that the dwarves who play the dancing Druids tower over it.

Michael's expression of utter disbelief as the miniature Stonehenge is lowered from the rafters is perfect. Backstage after the show, David finds the words to express what he was thinking: "I do not, for one, think that the band was down. I think that the problem may have been that there was a Stonehenge monument on the stage that was in danger of being crushed by a dwarf!"

Stonehenge, the real one, was at the center of one of my favorite "life imitates Spinal Tap" moments, when Black Sabbath went out on tour to promote their 1983 album, *Born Again.* The album happens to include a two-minute instrumental titled "Stonehenge." This inspired the band's manager, Don Arden—the father-in-law of Ozzy Osbourne, who had been fired as Sabbath's lead singer a few years earlier—to commission a towering Stonehenge set for the tour.

But the designers misunderstood the measurements, reading them in meters rather than feet, the result being that Sabbath was overshadowed by an unwieldy, humongous Stonehenge. In addition, Arden had hired a little person to dress up as the grotesque "devil baby" figure on the album's cover and lurk creepily around the stage. One night, the devil-baby actor took a fall from the oversized Stonehenge set and was badly injured.

When our film was released just weeks after Sabbath started their tour, the band, in a dimwitted Spinal Tap–like fit of pique, claimed that we had stolen the Stonehenge idea from them. All they needed was to do the math to realize that their accusation was ridiculous. Their tour took place nearly a year *after* we had wrapped *This Is Spinal Tap*. So unless we had access to H. G. Wells's time machine, there is no way we could have stolen the idea, shot the film, edited it, and had it in theaters right after Black Sabbath went on their Stonehenge tour.

In another life-imitates-Tap scenario, in *Heartbreakers Beach Party*, a documentary about Tom Petty made by Cameron Crowe at the same time we were making *This Is Spinal Tap*, there's a scene in which Petty and his band get lost en route to the stage. Wandering in the bowels of a huge German entertainment complex, they open what they presume to be the stage door, only to find themselves standing on an indoor tennis court.

There have since been many instances in which *This Is Spinal Tap* hasn't just imitated life—it's anticipated it. In 1991, Metallica put out an album with an all-black cover. In 1992, Jeff Porcaro, the drummer of Toto, tragically died in, wait for it, a bizarre gardening accident. He had a heart attack that was brought on by the pesticides he was using. And in 1997, the members of U2, while on their elaborate PopMart tour, got stuck inside a giant lemon prop onstage.

We were careful to have Spinal Tap live in a parallel universe. Tap was not modeled on a specific band. It was an amalgam of a number of bands and solo artists. People assumed that Chris modeled Nigel on Jeff Beck, who also had a pageboy haircut, or that Harry modeled Derek on Black Sabbath bassist Geezer Butler, who also had long dark hair and a handlebar mustache. But Chris, Harry, and Michael were simply allowing the heavy metal world to enter their creative consciousnesses and guide their choices.

The only instance where the real world collides with Tap's is during an exchange between Ian and Bobbi Flekman, where a reference to the Beatles is made when Bobbi says, "I don't think that a sexy cover is the answer for why an album sells or doesn't sell. 'Cause you tell me: *The White Album*—what was that? There was nothing on that goddamned cover." And the only explicit mentions of actual recording artists are when Tommy talks about Frank Sinatra in his limo and when David, Nigel, and Derek visit Elvis's grave.

Outside of those exceptions, we were committed to keeping Tap in its own world. But we did have our disagreements about some things. As close to the bone as we were with the satire, I always felt that there had to be an emotional component to the story. Initially, I got some pushback on that—and I understood why. Satire and emotion have never been known to peacefully coexist. The nature of satire is to make fun of things, call people out, shine a spotlight on bullshit. But I've always felt that it's not enough to say what you're against; you also have to say what you're for. I wanted the film, even if in a small way, to reflect that.

It's a difficult balancing act. I struggled with the same thing a few years later when I made *The Princess Bride*. Yes, it's a satire of swashbuckling movies. But it's also a love story, which makes for strange bedfellows. In *This Is Spinal Tap*, the heart lies in the connection between Nigel and David. They have been best friends since they were boys, and music is their bond. So after Nigel storms off the stage at the air force base and then shows up backstage before the now Tufnel-less band is about to go on at a concert hall in Los Angeles, I felt we had a good moment to weave in the emotional element.

Our treatment originally had Nigel crashing the stage on his own, essentially willing himself back into the band. But that didn't feel earned. So the way we had it play out is Nigel pays them a surprise visit and offhandedly informs them that "Sex Farm" has charted in the top ten in Japan. David, still bitter, rejects Nigel's attempt at reconciliation. As the band leaves to take the stage, Nigel is left alone in the dressing room. It's one of my favorite shots in the movie, visually and emotionally.

When the band hits the stage, Nigel wanders into the wings. David notices him there. After a few bars of "Tonight I'm Gonna Rock You Tonight," David starts to feel the pull of their long friendship. He beckons Nigel to rejoin the band onstage.

There was some initial resistance within our ranks to this idea. The concern was that we were breaking a cardinal rule of satire: no happy endings.

But I think we were able to strike the right balance. We turned the EMOTION knob to about four. But with Tap's drummer exploding onstage almost immediately thereafter, we kept the SATIRE knob at eleven.

In the movie's triumphant final scene, not counting the interview clips during the credits, Tap is seen playing to an adoring Japanese audience. We shot this scene at Perkins Palace in Pasadena, which doubled for a venue in Tokyo called Kobe Hall. Chris wore a Yomiuri Giants baseball jersey with Sadaharu Oh's number on it. The auditorium was decked out with *Nisshōki*, the red-on-white flag of Japan. (If you look closely, you can see that the flags still have the fold marks on them from the packaging they came in. We were so pressed for time that we didn't have time to iron them.)

And with Tap's triumphs in "Japan," the shoot was over. Now all that was left to do was to take the forty-plus hours of raw footage, cut it down to something that made sense, and hope the studio would like it.

CHAPTER 9

# How Can I Leave This Behind?

There's an old saying that goes, "How do you make a sculpture of an elephant? You chip away everything that's not an elephant."

So began the task of turning our forty-plus hours of footage into a movie elephant. The process took a solid nine months. Although we had a basic storyline, there was no written script to serve as a road map. It was like trying to put together a jigsaw puzzle with no picture on the box. There were sometimes three or four versions of a scene. The challenge was to take the best of each version and figure out how to stitch them together into something that made sense and tracked. Essentially, we were "writing" with the pieces of film.

When you work with great improvisers, you end up with a mother lode of comedic gifts. Many times they can be used to button a scene. For example, at the end of Fred Willard's rambling monologue at the air force base, he said to the band, "I have just one request. Could you play a couple of slow numbers, so I can dance?"

This was a perfect gazinta ("goes into") for the scene in which Tap plays "Sex Farm" to a hangar full of irritated military couples who are plugging their ears.

There are also serendipitous moments where you luck into a great transition. In the final scene of the film, we cut from Tap's drummer in America, Mick Shrimpton, to the new drummer in Japan, Joe "Mama" Besser. To reveal Joe "Mama," we set off an explosion from a flash pot in front of him. Then we discovered that when we cut from Mick to Joe, it looked as if *Mick* had exploded, just like Stumpy Joe's successor, Peter "James" Bond, who spontaneously combusted at the Isle of Lucy Jazz-Blues Festival. The movie gods had smiled down on us.

The first rough assembly of the film was over four hours long. And that didn't even include the three hours of interview footage we had shot. Needless to say, tough decisions had to be made. We debated over how much concert footage we should include. The guys felt we needed more. I felt less. The concert scenes, in my view, had to serve three functions: first, they had to show that these guys could really play, which they can; second, they had to be funny, either through the songs' lyrics or a physical gag; and third, they had to keep the film moving forward—we needed to see the band in performance but not let any performance overstay its welcome.

Ultimately, I think we struck the right balance. The only songs that play all the way through are "Big Bottom" and "Rock 'n' Roll Creation." And for the right reasons—the lyrics to "Big Bottom" are sustainably funny and the performance ends with the perfect visual, of David and Derek spanking Nigel on the tush with the necks of their bass guitars. And we designed "Rock 'n' Roll Creation" to pay off at the end, with Derek finally emerging from his pod only to hastily attempt to get back into it.

Early on in editing, it became obvious that some plotlines would have to be thrown out altogether. For example, originally, Spinal Tap had an opening act, a new wave band called the Dose. The guys are against having the Dose tour with them. They feel the group's punky music isn't a good fit with heavy metal. But then, during a sound check, they catch sight of the Dose's lead singer, Stellazine, played by Cherie Currie, the former lead singer of the Runaways—a beautiful, sexy young blonde in a skintight, metallic-blue catsuit.

After a deliberation of about an eighth of a second, the band does a one-eighty and insists to Ian that it's critical the Dose be their opening act for the entire length of the tour. Ian obliges and books the band. But there's a problem. Stellazine is what one might call a free spirit. After a scene in which Nigel is seen making time with her, he turns up with a herpes sore on his lip. Next, we see David pairing up with Stellazine, after which he, too, sports a herpes sore. Stellazine then proceeds to hang out with Derek and then Viv, both of whom subsequently also display the herpes badge.

A band meeting is called and a vote is taken: Should the Dose remain on the tour? The four herpes-inflicted Tap members vote the Dose out. Mick, who is clueless and herpes-free, votes for the Dose to stay.

Cherie's scenes were terrific, but the traveling herpes show took way too long to play out. So unfortunately, the sequence had to go. Only a fragment of it survives as a DVD extra in the Criterion Collection edition of *This Is Spinal Tap*. There is, however, a remnant of this subplot in the scene where Nigel and David defend the *Smell the Glove* album cover to Bobbi Flekman. Nigel has a sore on his lower lip, and David has one on his upper lip. Conspicuous as these blemishes are, they go unexplained. Depending on your take, this is either a complete non sequitur or an ambiguous "What the hell is going on?" moment. Either way, it always got a laugh—which surprised me.

We also abandoned a side trip into David's personal life where it is revealed that, as a result of a fling he had years ago with a groupie, he has a son named Jordan St. Hubbins. Jordan, now a teenager, lives with his mother in Phoenix and has rebelled by becoming a punk rocker. This upsets David and leads to a backstage father-son confrontation. "The actor playing my son was Sean Frye, brother of Soleil Moon Frye of *Punky Brewster* fame," Michael recalls. "But the squabble at the venue and David's disapproval of the kid's appearance just didn't land right."

**F**or similar reasons, we ditched a sequence that showed Tap, after their "Jazz Odyssey" fiasco as a four-piece, trying to carry on with a new guitarist. Says Michael, "We had this scene where we get a replacement guitarist for Nigel, a kid named Ricky. He's only nineteen, and he comes in and just plays the shit out of 'Hell Hole.' He's really good, incredibly good-looking, and he's all over the stage. Jeanine keeps looking at him lustfully. At one point, Ricky lifts up his guitar in a pose and it hits me in the face. After that, he's out. It's a really cool scene in its own way, but it had no intro or outro, and that was the problem. Where did he come from? Do we have to see him auditioning? We didn't have time to get into all that."

Ricky, incidentally, was played by a musician named Louie Merlino, who has since done hundreds of sessions as a backup singer and now lives in Las Vegas.

There was also a subplot about Derek going through a painful divorce. We filmed a number of scenes of Derek on the phone, getting the latest bad news from his lawyer. In one scene, he learns that his soon-to-be ex has taken out a full-page ad in the *New Musical Express* laying out her settlement demands. In another, Derek is seen saying, "She can't have the Lamborghini . . . Okay, she *can* have the Mini." Again, it slowed the momentum. So the audience would never learn of Derek's crumbling marriage.

Ric Parnell, who had no background in acting, delivered an incredible performance in a scene we cut. The setup was that Artie Fufkin had succeeded in getting the band to do the early-morning radio station appearance. What Artie didn't know was that, on that day, the station had only just changed its programming format from sports talk to rock 'n' roll. One caller, who wasn't aware of the change, asks the band, "Can you settle a bet I have with a buddy of mine? I think Ferguson Jenkins had fifty shutouts with the Cubs. He says he had forty-four. Who's right?" Just as the radio host is about to brush off the question, Mick Shrimpton, shades on, cigarette in hand, answers: "Neither. Neither of you guys are right. Ferguson Jenkins has had forty-eight career shutouts, and they weren't all with Chicago."

Then, in his sleepy drawl, he proceeds to deliver a complete statistical breakdown of Jenkins's career. But since we ended up losing the radio station scene, we lost with it Ric Parnell's eloquent Ferguson Jenkins soliloquy.

I not only cut scenes we had planned. On any given day, brilliant stuff would spontaneously fly out of someone's mouth. A lot of that stuff had to go, too, to keep the film's motor running. In particular, I remember a dissertation that David delivered to Marty about slime molds:

> Slime molds are so close to being both plant and animal that it's like they can't make up their mind. They're thinking now that maybe this is who's been running the earth all this time: these layabouts who can't commit.
>
> 'Cause there's more slime molds than any other form of protoplasm on the planet. And if they wanted to—if they finally made up their minds to commit to being either plant or animal—they could take us over like that. You're walking down an alleyway. You slip and twist your ankle, maybe. It wasn't an accident. It was an attack.

There was also Nigel's devotion to the stop-motion character Gumby, a melding of Nigel and Chris. "I always liked Gumby," Chris says. "I wrote to Art Clokey, who had created him, and he wrote back, which was just insane. I wanted his permission to use the character and the T-shirt. We had a real correspondence for a while. He would send me handwritten letters and draw little Gumby and Pokey figures at the top of them, sometimes with little speech bubbles that said things like 'Hi, Christopher!'"

On the set of *This Is Spinal Tap*, 1982: Derek Smalls (Harry Shearer), Nigel Tufnel (Christopher Guest), David St. Hubbins (Michael McKean), and director Rob (not Marty DiBergi) Reiner. MARY EVANS/RONALD GRANT/EVERETT COLLECTION

*Top:* Rob as radio deejay Wolfman Jack introducing Spinal Tap to the world on *The TV Show*, 1979. *Bottom:* The first iteration of the band, from left: Michael McKean, Loudon Wainwright III (keyboards), Harry Shearer, Christopher Guest, and Russ Kunkel (drums). COLUMBIA PICTURES TELEVISION

Rob as documentarian Marty DiBergi in his signature USS OORAL SEA baseball cap, with his never-used viewfinder. PHOTO COURTESY OF AUTHORIZED SPINAL TAP LLC

Roger Grimsby, an anchor for WABC's *Eyewitness News* in New York, in an undated promotional handout. The backs of these promo cards, acquired by Harry via his then girlfriend, Jane Wallace, proved useful for jotting down scene ideas for *This Is Spinal Tap*. An idea's worthiness was determined by passing the "Does this deserve a Grimsby?" test. WABC

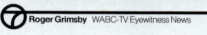

From a deleted scene, Spinal Tap at their first U.S. press conference: drummer Eric "Stumpy Joe" Childs (Russ Kunkel), lead guitarist Nigel Tufnel, lead singer David St. Hubbins, and bassist Derek Smalls. MPTV IMAGES

The first scene shot for the movie: a flashback of Spinal Tap tapping into the zeitgeist by performing "(Listen to the) Flower People" on American TV in 1967. ALAMY IMAGES

"And oh, how they danced . . ." The band with David's girlfriend, Jeanine Pettibone (June Chadwick), their manager, Ian Faith (Tony Hendra), and the "Druids" (Chris Romano and Daniel Rodgers) on the day the "Stonehenge" sequence was shot. MPTV IMAGES

Manager Ian Faith and the band pose with Polymer Records president Sir Denis Eton-Hogg (Patrick Macnee). EVERETT COLLECTION

Rob directs June Chadwick and Michael in the disastrous in-store promo scene that prompted Artie Fufkin (Paul Shaffer) to tell the band, "Kick my ass." MPTV IMAGES

In a scene that was cut from the film, Nigel, David, and Tap groupies take great pleasure in watching their marijuana-imbued chauffeur, Tommy Pischedda (Bruno Kirby), channel his idol Frank Sinatra with a pizza-crust microphone. MPTV IMAGES

Derek, Nigel, Mick Shrimpton (Ric Parnell), Viv Savage (David Kaffinetti), and David at the Beachwood Canyon faux castle that stood in for Nigel's baronial estate. ALAMY IMAGES

Amid Nigel's collection of rare guitars, Marty and Nigel discuss the latter's possible future as a salesman in a men's chapeau shop. ALAMY IMAGES

Harry as Derek, strutting and strumming his stuff...
HENRY DILTZ PHOTOGRAPHY

... followed by the indignity of an airport security officer (Gloria Gifford) screening him for his semi-hidden "stuff."
EVERETT COLLECTION

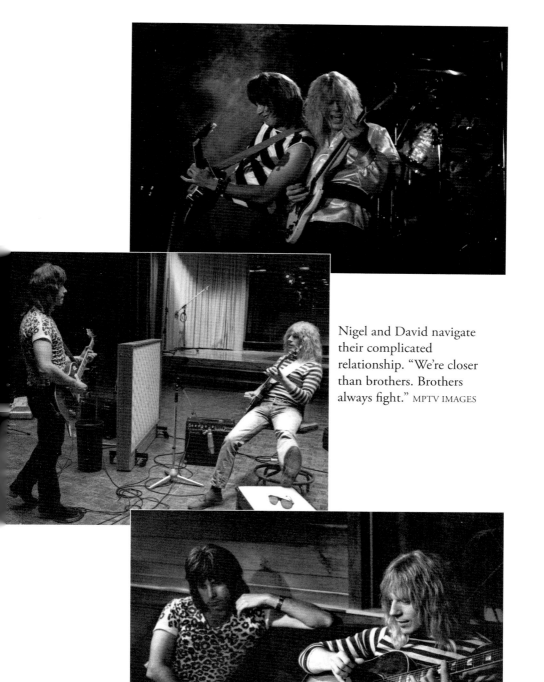

Nigel and David navigate their complicated relationship. "We're closer than brothers. Brothers always fight." MPTV IMAGES

First-time director Rob Reiner introduces the trailer for *This Is Spinal Tap*—which, because the studio couldn't figure out how to market the movie, had nothing to do with the film. It features Chris, Harry, and Michael in full Alpine regalia in a short film about a cheese-rolling contest.
PHOTOS COURTESY OF AUTHORIZED SPINAL TAP LLC

Michael, Harry, and Christopher photographed for *Rolling Stone*, 1984. It was this photo, in particular the guy on the right, that caught the eye of a young actress named Jamie Lee Curtis. AARON RAPOPORT PHOTOGRAPHY

Spinal Tap performing at CBGB in New York City, 1984. ROBIN PLATZER PHOTOGRAPHY

Spinal Tap back on the road in 1992. HENRY DILTZ PHOTOGRAPHY

At the Tower Bridge in London for the "Majesty of Rock" video shoot, 1992. NEWS UK/NEWS LICENSING

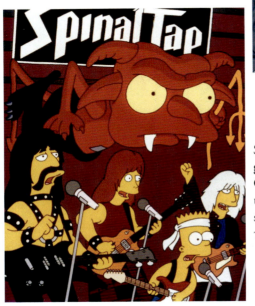

Spinal Tap, with Bart, makes a guest appearance on *The Simpsons*. Over the years, Harry has provided upward of twenty-five voices for the show. *THE SIMPSONS* © AND ™ 1990 20TH TELEVISION. ALL RIGHTS RESERVED.

Christopher, Harry, Michael, and Rob reunite for a thirty-fifth-anniversary screening of *This Is Spinal Tap* at the 2019 Tribeca Film Festival. DIA DIPASUPIL/ GETTY IMAGES FOR TRIBECA FILM FESTIVAL

Scenes from Spinal *Tap II: The End Continues* . . . Marty DiBergi tracks down Artie Fufkin (Paul Shaffer), erstwhile Polymer Records promotion man turned salesman of "dancing inflatables."

Former Tap publicist Bobbi Flekman (Fran Drescher), today a manager of social media influencers, explains to Marty the calming role that Buddhism now plays in her life.

Derek gets tips on how to get back into rockin' shape from fitness guru Bob Kitness of Kitness Fitness (John Michael Higgins). ALL PHOTOS THIS PAGE COURTESY OF CASTLE ROCK

Spinal Tap 2025: CJ "Caucasian Jeff" Vanston (keyboards), Valerie "Didi Crockett" Franco (drums), Nigel, David, and Derek with Marty on location in New Orleans. The pose is an homage to Crosby, Stills & Nash's first album cover; both shots were taken by the legendary rock photographer Henry Diltz.
HENRY DILTZ PHOTOGRAPHY

Marty interviews Sir Paul McCartney (as himself) for *Spinal Tap II*. COURTESY OF CASTLE ROCK

"When we're ashes, we'll still be bashing." David, Derek, and Nigel rock on with frenemy documentarian Marty DiBergi. HENRY DILTZ PHOTOGRAPHY

On a whim, we shot a scene where Nigel talks back to the television while watching a Gumby cartoon. In another scene we cut, the band discusses their plan to go to Graceland to visit Elvis's grave. Nigel, with his toy Gumby tucked into the breast pocket of his shirt, bends Gumby's head as a show of respect to the King. In the completed film, you'll notice Gumby in Nigel's pocket in the "Cups and Cakes" scene.

It's easy to become self-indulgent. You fall in love with stuff that makes you laugh and you want to leave it in even though it doesn't help sculpt the elephant. But you have to be ruthless. If you indulge, you lose the audience.

So we sculpted away. Originally, the scene where the band gets lost trying to find the stage had more dialogue between the band and the maintenance man who gives them directions (played by a terrific actor named Wonderful Smith). We had a bit where Nigel positions himself in a fixed spot, shouting, "Hello! Hello!" so the other guys would have a reference point to prevent them from getting even more lost. But this took away from a more important bit, the band's efforts to amp themselves up for the crowd. (It was in this spirit that Harry shouted out a line that became one of the film's most quoted: "Hello, Cleveland!")

The "Australian's nightmare" scene, where Ian ridicules Jeanine and quits, used to include a series of filthy comebacks improvised by June, with Jeanine calling Ian a "bumbling dwarf-willied prick," a "fucking twit full of shit," and an "impotent bat 'n' balls full o' crabs."

As tempting as it was to leave these moments in, all they did was grow the elephant a second trunk. When it came to the scenes we shot depicting the seamy "sex and drugs" side of rock 'n' roll, we made the decision to play that aspect down. There is a fleeting moment where you can see some groupies sniffing powder. But we cut all the other scenes showing drug use and a moment where Nigel has his arm around a topless girl. We felt it went against the tone of the film.

For me, looking back after forty years, all I see are the flaws that stayed in the movie, such as the continuity mistakes that I would avoid in a scripted film. With an improvised film, there are times when you just have to live with mismatches. For instance, in the scene where the band reacts to the all-black cover of the *Smell the Glove* album, you'll notice that Nigel's position keeps changing from shot to shot. First, we see him standing to the right of Ian Faith. Then, after a cut to David and Jeanine, we go back to Nigel, who is now standing to Ian's left as he observes, "It's so black, it's like, how much more black could this be? And the answer is: None. None more black." Normally, you want to avoid that kind of gaffe. But it was the only take where Chris said, "None more black," so we lived with it.

Few viewers pick up on this stuff. The editor Bob Leighton, with whom I worked on this and many of my other films, has always said that it's more important to make the audio work smoothly than the visuals. A jump in sound is much more jarring than a jump in picture. If the dialogue is flowing, it'll paper over visual mismatches. (A little side note: You can hear Bob's voice near the beginning of the film. When the roadies are loading in the band's giant horned skull, a voice tells them, "Watch his mouth. Watch his mouth." We added that line in postproduction.)

Originally, to give the film a matching set of bookends, I had Marty address the camera at the end the way he does in the opening. He explains what happened to Tap after their Tokyo triumph: another breakup, followed by another re-formation, this time with a drummer named Nicky Pepys, the son of their original drummer, John "Stumpy" Pepys.

Though this would have proven remarkably prescient—in 2007, Led Zeppelin would reunite with Jason Bonham, the son of their late drummer, John Bonham—Marty's epilogue just didn't feel right. It was much better to leave Tap in their moment of serendipitous triumph, with their next steps entirely in the audience's imagination. So one last cut was made.

# CHAPTER 10

# It's Not Too Late

In the fall of '83, I delivered an eighty-three-minute cut of *This Is Spinal Tap* to the folks at Embassy and awaited a response that I hoped would be "You're a genius. You've made the *Citizen Kane* of fake documentaries."

This was not to be the case.

Had I known how unenthusiastic the response would be, I'm not sure I'd have been able to make it through the nine-month editing period. Thankfully, Lindsay Doran had insulated me from it. "I was pretty much the lone champion of the movie," she says. "It always felt to me like I was Don Quixote."

Late in 1983, Embassy arranged for two out-of-town preview screenings: the first in Dallas, the second in Seattle. The idea was that Dallas would give us an idea of how the movie would play in the heartland, while Seattle would give us more of a college-town read. Michael recalls that in Dallas, we were sandwiched between test previews of the sci-fi adventure movies *Krull* and *Yor*—the perfect companions to a satirical documentary about a fictional rock band.

To say that the results in Dallas were disastrous would be kind. Lindsay recalls, "Nobody was laughing. They laughed at the physical stuff—when Derek was caught in the pod, when the band got lost backstage. But otherwise, silence. They didn't laugh at the verbal jokes at all."

Worse than that, the movie failed to hold the audience's attention. During the screening, people wandered in and out of the theater to get popcorn, smoke cigarettes, and chat in the lobby before going back in, if they went back in at all.

The chatter we overheard from audience members afterward was equally disconcerting. "It was clear that many people thought this was a straight documentary," Chris recalls. "I heard two girls saying to each other, 'These guys are so stupid!'"

After the screening, I was approached by someone who asked, "Why would you make a movie about a band that nobody's ever heard of, and one that's so bad?" Someone else complained about the shaky, amateurish camerawork.

Then came the comment cards. "I was in a hotel room in Dallas when some Embassy guy came in with a box of cards and dumped them on the coffee table in front of me and the other Embassy people," says Lindsay. "He said, 'Just as I predicted, it was a disaster.'"

It was almost as if Embassy was rooting for the film to fail. This was my first experience with comment cards. As I read through them, a sense of doom came over me. But as I looked through what the respondents had written on the cards, I discovered something that I never knew. Apparently there are four alternative ways to spell the word *movie*: "movey," "movy," "movee," and, my favorite, "move." So there you have it. A crowd of geniuses. But however poorly educated these moviegoers were, we couldn't deny that our scores were terrible. As a general rule for a first test screening, if you average is somewhere in the seventies, that's okay. After you make some tweaks in response to the feedback, you can possibly get your scores into the eighties or higher. Then you're on your way.

*This Is Spinal Tap* scored in the forties.

"I've been in the movie business now for forty years, and I've been in hundreds and hundreds of previews. I've still never seen scores as bad as that," says Lindsay.

Still, we had high hopes for Seattle. I went with Bob Leighton back to the cutting room. We tightened up some spots that felt slow—nothing big, but enough to make things move a little better. I was confident Seattle would get it. "But somehow," says Michael, "all of those people from Dallas followed us to Seattle and scored the movie exactly the same as they had before."

**W**e were still in the forties. "That was really the end of it," says Lindsay. "Any money that Embassy was going to put into it for marketing and publicity disappeared."

The poster that Embassy came up with added insult to our already injured psyches. The poster—or "one sheet," as it's called—was a cartoon drawing of a guitar whose neck was tied in a knot. It was a direct rip-off of the poster for the 1980 hit comedy *Airplane!*, which featured a plane twisted into a knot. No disrespect to *Airplane!*, a very funny movie, but Embassy's art screamed of desperation: *Hey, maybe we can sell this stinker as the next* Airplane!

"Oh, they had no fucking clue," says Chris. "They didn't get it in the beginning, they didn't get it when it came out, and they wouldn't ever get it, basically. Any claims after the fact are bullshit. These people were looking at us and saying, 'I don't know what this is.'"

"We were in shaky hands," says Harry. "The year we were filming, the only movies Embassy had in release were called *Paradise* and *Parasite*. They knew that those letters in some combination meant money, but they didn't know quite what the combination was."

Embassy set a release date of March 2, 1984. But as the day approached, we knew that since they weren't going to be particularly supportive, our only hope was to mount a guerrilla campaign to try to get the word out ourselves.

In keeping with the tone of our film, we decided that, rather than go out with a traditional trailer showing clips from the movie, we'd do something a bit different. We created a "trailer" that opens with me in the editing room, holding up the two Emmys I won for *All in the Family* and talking directly into the camera. I explain to the audience waiting for the feature to start that the studio insisted we show a trailer to promote the film. But since I am still busy editing, I tell them I am going to instead share with them a short film I found lying around that I think they might enjoy.

Then I switch on a 16mm projector and a scratchy, seemingly old film starts to play. The first thing you see is a silhouetted man blowing an eight-foot-long horn, accompanied by *National Geographic*–style narration by our resident voice-over maven, Harry Shearer: "The call of the alpenhorn echoes across the Danskin Peninsula, the heart of Denmark's cheese belt!"

What follows is a short "documentary," directed by Harry, about an entirely fictitious cheese-rolling festival. The inspiration for this came from Chris, who had read an article somewhere about a cheese-rolling contest in which a man was allegedly crushed to death by a runaway wheel of Gouda. "In every glen and fjord," announces Harry's cheery narrator, "three days are set aside at the end of every other April, or *Unter-Apvel*, for a joyous celebration of cheese!"

This "celebration" was filmed in a park near the CBS Studio Center in the San Fernando Valley. In the film, Michael, Chris, Harry, and our actor friends appear dressed up in vaguely Alpine garb—lederhosen, dirndls, tasseled stocking caps—and engage in rolling giant wheels of cheese down a hill. We also showed additional activities that included cheese: cheese-discus throwing, cheese-blowing (à la glassblowing), and the competitive stuffing of cheese down one's pants. If you look closely, you might spot a little boy who grew up to be Jake Gyllenhaal. Well, he already was Jake Gyllenhaal; he just became a more famous Jake Gyllenhaal. We were friends with his parents, director Stephen Gyllenhaal and screenwriter Naomi Foner, and they were more than happy to loan out their son. Maggie, Jake's sister, tagged along, too. The film ends with a man (Ed Begley Jr.) and a woman (P. J. Soles of *Rock 'n' Roll High School* fame) being crowned the King and Queen of Cheese.

In our minds, this was the perfect trailer for *This Is Spinal Tap*. If the audience dug this, they would dig our film.

To help promotion, the band recorded an original soundtrack album of all the songs in the film, which we released with a black album cover. Chris directed an MTV-style video for "Hell Hole," complete with scantily clad women and a skeletal hand of death that, at the end, sweeps away tiny models of the band members. We thought, "Maybe, if we get lucky, MTV will put the video in heavy rotation alongside Def Leppard's 'Photograph.'"

I arranged advance screenings of the film for the *Los Angeles Times* and *Rolling Stone* in hopes of getting a drumbeat going. And they liked what they saw. The *L.A. Times* guy worried that the spoof might be "too close for comfort," but added, "With the help of an upcoming MTV video and soundtrack album, Reiner is convinced that all but the most brain-damaged metal fans will get the joke." *Rolling Stone* ran an item in their "Random Notes" column in February that said, "Reiner is counting on word-of-mouth to tip off the hoi polloi to the movie before its March premiere."

The truth is, there was no premiere. No red carpet. No fanfare whatsoever. The movie just . . . came out.

"I asked Embassy to send me to New York for opening weekend because it felt like there was a child graduating from elementary school and no parent was going to be there," Lindsay says. "I literally stood on street corners and handed out pamphlets."

*This Is Spinal Tap* opened at the 57th Street Playhouse and three other theaters in New York. "I went to them all," Lindsay says. "They were definitely not full."

To put a fine point on it: we were fucked.

# CHAPTER 11

# Yes, Please, Sir, and Thank You, Ma'am

Somehow, our opening was not the unmitigated disaster we had braced ourselves for. The reviews were for the most part ecstatic—as if we had written them ourselves. In the *Fort Worth Star-Telegram*, Dave Hickey, a fine-art writer as well as film critic, called it "the funniest movie ever made about rock 'n' roll"—words echoed verbatim by David Ansen of *Newsweek*.

Two weeks after we opened, Vincent Canby, the *New York Times*'s senior film critic, wrote a long think piece in which he called the film "a movie of such high-class nuttiness that I suspect it might prove as entertaining to audiences who've never seen a rock-concert film as to those who take their rock very seriously." It felt like semi-vindication. At least we were a hit with people who knew how to spell "movie."

And though we didn't open big, word-of-mouth was positive and our grosses increased slightly from week to week. In the more cosmopolitan cities like Boston, Chicago, New York, and L.A., the film played for months. Although the overall box office was not, as *Variety* would put it, boffo, by the end of our theatrical run in the U.S., in the summer of '84, we had grossed $4.5 million, essentially twice what it had cost to make the film.

What Embassy failed to take into account was that there were people out there who were hip to the same pop-culture tropes and references that we were. Hickey observed, "The more you know about rock 'n' roll, the funnier this movie gets." Janet Maslin of the *New York Times* said, "There's an in-joke quality to the film, one that will make it all the more hilarious to anyone at all knowledgeable about either the aesthetic or the business aspects of pop music."

*This Is Spinal Tap*, a movie about less-than-genius rockers, made its viewers feel smart. We didn't become rich from the initial run—or, for that matter, from any subsequent VHS or DVD versions, or from foreign sales. But at least we felt good that our movie was finding an audience.

The only bad review of any significance came from John Mendelsohn, who wrote for the music magazine *Creem*. With the arrogance of the classic rock snob who knows better than anyone else how anything rock-related should be done, he called the film "a self-indulgent bore, a maddening exercise in squandered opportunities . . . If you started right now, it would be lunchtime tomorrow before you could list even half the heavy metal clichés the film should have poked fun at but doesn't." On and on Mendelsohn went in this vein. He could have saved himself some time by simply typing two words: "Shit sandwich."

Then, as our otherwise unanimously glowing reviews continued to pour in, *Creem* did a one-eighty in a July '84 review of the soundtrack album, praising "Marty DiBergi's masterful cinema vérité."

Chris, Michael, and Harry did everything they could to keep the movie alive. They appeared in character on *The Joe Franklin Show*, a local-TV New York City institution whose host, more accustomed to interviewing old vaudevillians and Tin Pan Alley types, accepted them at face value as a real British band.

> JOE: Did you begin *gigging*, as they say, in local pubs?
>
> DAVID, *in off-duty oversize Michael Caine eyeglasses*: Mostly outside of Tube stations. Subway stops.

They also appeared as the musical guests on the next-to-last show of *Saturday Night Live*'s ninth season. That week's host, Barry Bostwick, did a pretaped interview with the band in which he asked them about the new song they were premiering on *SNL*, "Christmas with the Devil."

> BARRY: Are you seriously interested in devil worship, or are you just using the trappings of Satanism to get attention?
>
> DEREK: I believe, and it goes for everybody in the band, that a man's relationship with the devil is a very private affair.
>
> BARRY: Some of your songs, like "Big Bottom," seem to portray women as sex objects, not as human beings. How do you feel about that?
>
> DAVID: We do not consider the subject of the song a human being at all, merely a part of one. Therefore, that gives us sort of a license to be as free as we want.

NIGEL: We are merely making, if you like, a scientific study of the bum.

A month later, NBC announced that Chris and Harry would be joining the *SNL* cast for the upcoming 1984–85 season. This was during the five-year period when Dick Ebersol took over for Lorne Michaels as executive producer. Chris's old friend Bob Tischler, formerly a producer of the *National Lampoon*'s record albums and radio programs, was, at the time, *SNL*'s head writer and de facto showrunner. "Ebersol was the executive in charge, but Bob was more like the producer," Chris says. "I had known him since 1970. He called me up and said, 'Would you guys want to come? You can basically do whatever you want. Really, do whatever the fuck you want to do.'"

Tischler wanted all three guys to join the cast, but Michael begged off. "I'd just gotten a new house and there was a baby on the way," he says. "It was not a time to leave L.A." Ebersol and Tischler went on to hire Billy Crystal, Martin Short, Rich Hall, and Pamela Stephenson to join a cast that already included Julia Louis-Dreyfus, Mary Gross, Jim Belushi, and Gary Kroeger. I think it may have been the strongest cast *SNL* has ever had.

Pre-*SNL* and pre-baby, Chris, Harry, and Michael, with David Kaffinetti and Ric Parnell, went out on an eight-city mini-tour to continue to promote the film and the soundtrack album. (Though Mick Shrimpton had exploded onstage, the guys rationalized Ric Parnell's appearance by saying that Mick's identical twin, Ric Shrimpton, had taken over his brother's drumming duties.)

In some cities, like Detroit, Spinal Tap received a relatively cool reception. But in Boston, where they played the Channel club on a rainy night—"It was also raining inside, and we were standing there with our electric instruments, thinking, 'Maybe this is where it ends,'" says Michael—they were received as gods.

"We were in a limo and they were trying to rock it," recalls Chris. "There were women baring their breasts at us when we played. That was a moment of 'Wait a minute, this is weird. Is this reality or are they just playing the role of a heavy metal audience?'"

Boston was by far the most Tap-mad city, and the only one in which the film played continuously for a solid year—ironic given that one of Tony Hendra's most famous lines in the film is "The Boston gig has been canceled. I wouldn't worry about it, though. It's not a big college town." Chris believes there may have been a causal relationship between these two things. "I wonder if Tony's line actually played a part in that," he says. "It's like when James Taylor sings, 'Now the first of December was covered with snow / So was the turnpike from Stockbridge to Boston,' and everyone in Massachusetts goes, 'Whooo! Yeah! He said it! He said the name of my town!'"

**T**he final show of the tour took place in Seattle, as part of that city's Bumbershoot festival. Seattle also became the final resting place for Tap's original horned skull. It had been shipped up from L.A. but mysteriously never came back. By this point, the band was getting a little tired of its limited repertoire.

"So we decided to play two Tap-ified covers we'd been messing around with at sound check, of Bruce Springsteen's 'Pink Cadillac' and Bobby Day's 'Rockin' Robin,'" recalls Michael. "The latter was sung by Chris as Nigel in raw, throaty fashion, with a very heavy arrangement. About seven years later, Seattle became the flash point for a new wave of heavy rock: Nirvana, Soundgarden, Pearl Jam,

Mudhoney, Screaming Trees. I rest my case. Spinal Tap invented grunge."

I would be remiss if I didn't acknowledge another domino effect of *This Is Spinal Tap*'s original release. In May of 1984, *Rolling Stone* ran an article about the movie and the band that included interviews with Chris, Michael, and Harry. Accompanying the article were photos of the guys both in character and as themselves. In the latter photo, they looked especially straight, with short hair and collared shirts. Harry's mustache was neatly trimmed, and Chris was genially resting his right arm on the shoulders of both Harry and Michael.

This photograph caught the eye of a young actress who had made her name in the John Carpenter horror films *Halloween* and *The Fog*, Jamie Lee Curtis. Jamie wasn't a regular *Rolling Stone* reader, but at the time, she was prepping for *Perfect*, a film adapted from a series of *Rolling Stone* articles that investigated the L.A. fitness-club scene. In the spring of '84, the latest issue, with the Spinal Tap article in it, was lying on her coffee table. Over to you, Jamie:

> I was sitting on a couch in my apartment in Colonial House, a beautiful old building in West Hollywood, with my friend Debra Hill, who was a writer and producer of *Halloween*. We were looking through an issue of *Rolling Stone* with Cyndi Lauper on the cover. There was a picture of three men, looking like regular dudes, all wearing button-up shirts.
>
> The guy on the right was smirking. I'm not a toothy-smile person. When my mother was pregnant with me, she had taken tetracycline, and as a result my teeth were always gray.

So I'd always been very self-conscious about my teeth and never smiled with my teeth ever. I recognized a fellow smirker. He was just handsome, he looked kind, and he had a smirk.

I said to Debra, "I'm going to marry him."

She said, "Who?"

I said, "The guy on the right. I'm going to marry him."

Debra said, "He's an actor. I tried to put him in a movie once. His name is Chris Guest."

For a third time, I said, "I'm going to marry him."

I had never seen *This Is Spinal Tap* or anything else Chris had been in. I found out through Debra that his agent was David Hoberman at ICM. The next day, I called David Hoberman. He picked up and said, "Hi, Jamie, I know all about it—Chris Guest. Debra Hill called me this morning."

Well, now I was mortified. I was embarrassed that Debra had done that. But I said, "I think the guy's cute. Here's my number. Have him call me if he wants." And Chris never called me.

Here's Chris's take:

My agent called me and said, "There's this person who wants you to have her number, Jamie Lee Curtis."

I said, "I don't know who that is." I hadn't seen *Halloween* or *The Fog*.

Eventually, I was having a meal with my friend Archie Hahn in a restaurant called Hugo's. Archie is the actor who plays the room-service guy in *This Is Spinal Tap*. I was sitting with Archie and there was a table across the way with three people sitting at it. Archie knew actors and said, "By the way, that's Jamie Lee Curtis."

Jamie continues:

So one day I picked up my friend Melanie Griffith and her then husband, Steven Bauer, in my Mustang convertible and we drove to Hugo's Restaurant on Santa Monica Boulevard. We got a table, and as I sat down, facing me, two tables away, was Chris, sitting with another man.

He didn't say anything. But he made a hand gesture of "Hi." I made the gesture back. Then I covered my mouth and said to my friends, "Oh my fucking God, there's the guy I left my number with, and he never called me." I was a little embarrassed.

Five minutes later, Chris was leaving. He stood up at his chair, shrugged his shoulders, and made a gesture of "Bye." He didn't come over. I sat in my chair, shrugged my shoulders, and made the same gesture.

That was June 28. But he called me the next day, June 29. We made a date to go out on July 2. We met at a restaurant called Chianti, on Melrose. We sat in a booth and Chris brought in his guitar because he had it in his car. We each had a glass of red wine. After dinner, we walked out onto the street and we made out on the sidewalk.

For July Fourth, he invited me over to Billy Crystal's house in the Pacific Palisades. We made out at Billy's house, a lot, but Chris didn't come home with me and I didn't go home with him.

If I may, I'd like to interject here: I happened to run into Jamie at another gathering earlier on that Fourth of July. I had no idea about her budding relationship with Chris. I flirted with her a bit and told her I was going over to Billy's later. Did she want to come with me?

Jamie said that she had already received an invitation. When I got to the party, I was stunned to find her there with Chris, engaging in, as the Brits would say, some heavy snogging. As Jamie recounts:

> Right after the Fourth, Chris went on tour with Spinal Tap for a week. When he came back, he invited me to a softball game he was playing in, somewhere in the Valley, with the Coney Island Whitefish. Right as I was walking up to the back side of the field, there was a crack of a bat, and Chris made a diving catch and did a somersault on the ground. Then he stood up with the ball in his mitt, looked over at me, and said, "Oh, hey." A very smooth, cool move on his part. I went home with him that night.
>
> He was leaving for New York in August for *Saturday Night Live*. He called his agent to try to get out of it, but he couldn't. I went to New York to visit him once.
>
> He called me one day in September when I was back in L.A. I was on set, on a pay phone on the lot. He said he was coming for the weekend. I asked him what he had done that day.
>
> He said, "Well, I took a walk up Fifth Avenue. To Cartier. Do you like diamonds?"
>
> I was like, "Yeah, whatever."
>
> So he came to visit me when he had a week off from *SNL*. He was carrying a bag with a heavy box in it. I thought, "Oh,

did he get me a watch?" But inside the box was a very simple eternity ring. He didn't say anything. I put it on.

Then, about an hour later, I said to him, "What is this?"

He said, "I was hoping you would marry me."

At 4:30 p.m. on December 18, 1984, just five and a half months after their first date, Chris and Jamie got married at my house on Hazen Drive in Beverly Hills. It was a small, informal gathering of no more than fifty people. The wedding cake was decorated with two figures, a Russian nesting doll and a baseball catcher. The catering was done by Hugo's, the restaurant where they first met.

Among those present were Jamie's mother, Janet Leigh; her father, Tony Curtis; and the chairman of MCA and the last of Hollywood's old-time movie moguls, Lew Wasserman, who was Jamie's godfather. I found myself talking with Tony, who at one point looked around the room and realized that, for the first time, all six of his children from his three marriages (to date, as of '84) were gathered in one place. With a smile on his face, Tony, invoking his birth name, said, "Bernie Schwartz has been a very busy fellow."

Chris and Jamie have now been married for over forty years. Their union is one of the enduring legacies of *This Is Spinal Tap*. At the time, however, legacy was the last thing any of us were thinking about. We were thrilled with the movie's reception and thrilled all over again when it showed up on several lists of "The Ten Best Films of 1984."

But we were all moving on—Chris and Harry to *SNL*, Michael to acting in the movies *Clue* and *Light of Day*, and me to my next project as a director, *The Sure Thing*.

*The Sure Thing* was a college-age romantic comedy starring John Cusack and Daphne Zuniga. It had come my way via Lindsay Doran, my champion at Embassy. She had overseen the development of the script, by Steven L. Bloom and Jonathan Roberts, for Henry Winkler and Roger Birnbaum's production company, Monument Pictures. Though I was less than thrilled with how Embassy had marketed *This Is Spinal Tap*, I liked the idea of a youthful romantic comedy that was not just another dopey, *Porky's*-style teen sex romp. And I loved working with Lindsay. I was so grateful for how she had been in my corner, I cast her in *This Is Spinal Tap* as a partygoer in a scene toward the end of the film, shot on the roof of the Hyatt hotel on Sunset Strip. It's the one where David and Derek are discussing their desire to do a musical about Jack the Ripper called *Saucy Jack*.

*The Sure Thing* was warmly described by more than one reviewer as *It Happened One Night* for young people. I got to work with John, Daphne, Tim Robbins, Anthony Edwards, and my future producing and Castle Rock Entertainment partner, my good friend Andy Scheinman.

I can tell you that it doesn't get any better than working on a project with friends. If *The Sure Thing* was that, *This Is Spinal Tap* was that in spades. For all the agita we had endured to get the movie made and released, we loved the experience. We had made the movie we wanted to make, on our terms. Now it was time to end that chapter of our lives. At the time, none of us had any idea that *This Is Spinal Tap* would continue writing chapters beyond 1984.

CHAPTER 12

# I Rode the Jet Stream, I Hit the Top

"Is this the *real* Spinal Tap? British heavy metal band Saxon performed Friday night at the Santa Monica Civic before a full house of mostly teenage fans who apparently couldn't tell the difference between a party and a parody. The entire show was unintentionally hilarious, from the cheesy, man-the-battlements set to the even cheesier 30-foot, eagle-shaped lighting truss they hauled down every 20 minutes."

**T**his dismissive review, written by Don Waller, appeared in the *Los Angeles Times* on April 16, 1984, six weeks after our movie opened. I don't think Waller was even aware of the fact that Harry had studied the moves of Saxon's bass player. The significance of Waller's article is that it contains perhaps the earliest use of the words "Spinal Tap" as shorthand for "overblown rock music and inept showmanship" in a major publication.

Our film was seeping into the rock consciousness. We became

aware that real rock stars had seen the film. The feedback wasn't always positive, notes Michael: "In '86, I was doing the movie *Light of Day* in Chicago with Paul Schrader. Schrader's a big rock guy. He told me that he had been at some club where he ran into Ozzy Osbourne. Paul said, 'I told Ozzy I was working with Michael McKean. The name didn't ring a bell. Then I said, "From *This Is Spinal Tap*." And Ozzy said he didn't like the movie because it was too close to real life.' That was one of the first times I became aware of leakage of Spinal Tap into the real world."

A few years later, in a *New Musical Express* interview, Ozzy expanded upon his opinion: "Everybody was saying to me, you've got to see this film *This Is Spinal Tap*. I wasn't laughing! It was fucking real. It was fucking real, man. It's like a documentary, not a fucking funny film. That's *it*, man! That's what it's like!"

Steven Tyler, the lead singer of Aerosmith, was encouraged by the band's lead guitarist, Joe Perry, to see the film. "You've got to see this movie. It's so fucking good. It's hilarious," Perry told Tyler. Tyler did not have the same take. He felt like he was the butt of a joke. "That movie bummed me out," he said. "Because I thought, 'How dare they? That's all real. And they're mocking it.'"

In his first flush of rock stardom, Axl Rose of Guns N' Roses was even more combative, telling *Melody Maker* in 1987, "I never saw *Spinal Tap* when it came out. I read an interview where these guys said they wrote it after they read something about Iron Maiden calling themselves troubadours of rock 'n' roll. They thought it was fucking ridiculous. What do they mean, fucking ridiculous? These guys are in a band, they tour the fucking world, they're like a miniature army. That's their job."

Axl's bandmate Slash was a bit more generous. "We don't think we're in the Spinal Tap position," he said. "The movie's okay, though. When I saw the singer stand up and say, 'This is a beautiful ballad called "Lick My Love Pump,"' I thought, 'Yeah, it's okay after all.'"

The film did have some admirers whose opinions I really valued. Foremost was Marty Scorsese, whose wrath I feared, given that I'd appropriated his first name. Marty recalls that he first saw *This Is Spinal Tap* at a packed theater in Westwood shortly after its release. "It caught the feel of vérité documentary—the camera moves, the cutting, the way people talked on camera, which had become clichés at that point," he says. "It was a comedy but it didn't have gags, per se. Everything was very believable. The overall vérité ambience was as carefully done as the *War of the Worlds* broadcast or the 'News on the March' sequence in *Citizen Kane*."

Any sensitivity to the idea that he and *The Last Waltz* were being sent up was, Marty says, outweighed by the silliness of it all. "I did feel a little protective about rock 'n' roll itself, because the music was a transcendental force for me and millions of others—the best of it, that is," he says. "Were they really satirizing *all* rock music? That wasn't the point. They were definitely having fun with a certain *reverence* for the music. But the satire wasn't aimed at the great music. The *not*-so-great music, that whole rock 'n' roll milieu—that was the target."

Besides, says Marty, he never thought that I was specifically "doing" him. "You could look through many thousands of photographs of me over the years and you will *never* catch me wearing a baseball hat," he says. "Not *ever*."

And as time went by, we found that we had our share of allies in the rock world. The mid-eighties marked the golden age of charity records: "Do They Know It's Christmas?" by Band Aid, "We Are the World" by USA for Africa, "Sun City" by Artists United Against Apartheid. In the spring of '85, the heavy metal heavies followed suit. Ronnie James Dio, the diminutive, leather-lunged powerhouse who had been Ozzy's replacement in Black Sabbath, organized a session for a charity song he had cowritten called "Stars." The proceeds would go to famine relief in Africa. Dio named his metal supergroup Hear 'n Aid and invited dozens of hard rockers to attend, among them members of Judas Priest, Mötley Crüe, Iron Maiden, Quiet Riot, W.A.S.P., Dokken, . . . and Spinal Tap.

"Chris was busy and couldn't make it, but Harry and I went," says Michael. "The video is the only time you see Derek without facial hair, because it was too short notice for Harry to grow his mustache. But we got to hang out with these guys. Ronnie Dio was great. There was something cool about seeing this confident little bastard running the show. Everyone was really nice to us. I brought my son's bass and they all signed it for him."

The video presented a surreal tableau: all these guys with their hair teased to eighties heights, pumping their fists, bobbing their heads, holding their headphones tight to their ears . . . and, in their midst, Michael and Harry, wigged and wailing away, having crossed over into the real heavy metal universe.

"For Michael and me," Harry recalls, "it was the first exposure we had to the idea that the movie had grown a life. Some of the guys seemed to think that it was all real. Most of them, of course, knew better. We were the only ones wearing comedy wigs. That we knew of."

"We were being embraced," says Michael, "but still just in the hard-rock ghetto."

We appreciated the positive acknowledgments. We even appreciated being trashed by metalheads who thought the movie *wasn't fuckin' funny, man*. But we were convinced that the references to Tap in the music press and the rock world would die down in due time.

Due time never came.

Karen Murphy, our producer, sensed something was up when she visited London in 1985, during the heyday of the British electro-pop band Frankie Goes to Hollywood. To promote their hit single "Relax," the group had commissioned the designer Katharine Hamnett to create oversized white T-shirts emblazoned with the block-letter slogan FRANKIE SAY RELAX. Those T-shirts spawned tons of imitators. Karen spotted one on a young lad that read NIGEL SAY MINE GOES TO 11.

Then there was Lindsay Doran's encounter with Michael Lindsay-Hogg, the director of the Beatles' *Let It Be*. "He said that *This Is Spinal Tap* was basically the same movie," she says. "*Let It Be* was out of circulation at the time, and this was decades before Peter Jackson edited the extra footage into *Get Back*. Michael said the Spinal Tap members were acting out storylines they didn't even know had been cut from *Let It Be*."

This story has been verified by Michael Lindsay-Hogg himself: "It reminded me of *Let It Be* in that it went from guys who had started out at twenty-one or twenty-two and enjoyed success to older guys struggling to take on their next life. And I'm not talking just about the Beatles. I also worked with the Rolling Stones and the Who. I saw Roger Daltrey, Pete Townshend, and Keith Moon get into fistfights.

So when I watched *This Is Spinal Tap*, I thought, 'What crystal ball had these guys looked into? How were they able to invent or imagine things that had really happened?'"

**E**ngland took to Tap quicker and more deeply than America did. While we never had an opening-night screening in the U.S., the film's UK distributor flew Chris and Harry to London for its September 1984 premiere at the Electric Cinema, a beloved repertory house in Notting Hill. (Michael stayed home with his expectant wife.)

"We were a bit nervous about how they would take Americans playing Brits," admits Harry, "sort of internally cowering in advance of a barrage of 'How dare they?' But that was not at all the response. We were surprised and delighted by how popular we were over there."

In the eighties, the UK's music-savvy readers supported three rock weeklies, *New Musical Express*, *Melody Maker*, and *Sounds*. These publications and their faithful readers constantly referenced the movie. They appreciated how, to quote *NME*'s Cynthia Rose in a 1984 write-up, "American actors revenged themselves on the British Invasion by creating the perfect loser stage ensemble of all time."

Rose, no relation to our detractor Axl, was among the first to use the C-word—*cult*—in relation to our film, observing that in the UK, screenings of *This Is Spinal Tap* were "drawing more rabid cult crowds than anything since *Rocky Horror*."

An even bigger surprise hit us with the first issue of a glossy new British music monthly that was launched in the fall of '86. It was called *Q*. On its cover was Paul McCartney, who, in the course of his interview, reflected on the Beatles' feelings about Yoko Ono. "We didn't accept Yoko totally," he said, "but how many groups do you know who would? It's a joke, like Spinal Tap."

And there you have it. A Beatle knew about us.

A year later, George Harrison, straining to be gracious while assessing L.A.'s music scene, told *Creem*, "Gandhi said, 'Create and preserve the image of your choice,' so if you want to be Spinal Tap, then best of luck to you." Make that *two* Beatles.

The 1964 *Ed Sullivan Show*–watching teenagers in us were thrilled. Hell, so were the pushing-forty versions of us.

The biggest factor in extending the life of our film was the advent of the VCR. In 1982, when we were making the movie, home video was still in its early days. Only Hollywood insiders and rich people owned videocassette players. But by 1985, VCR prices had dropped and the industry took advantage. Blockbuster Video, the future national behemoth, opened its first store that year in Dallas. Smaller video-rental shops were popping up all over the country.

One of the pioneers in the home-video market was a man named Andre Blay. In 1977, his company, Magnetic Video, was the first to license the rights from Hollywood studios to release their films in VHS and Betamax formats. Five years later, when we were shooting *Tap*, Blay had become the head of Embassy Pictures' new home-video division. Unbeknownst to us at the time, Embassy had so little faith in our movie's potential earning power that, before *This Is Spinal Tap* had even been released theatrically, the studio had sold the home-video rights for next to nothing.

This was the first of many financial indignities we would endure. It would take us decades and a lawsuit to begin to right the ways we had been wronged. But Blay's expertise in home video made our film available to a much bigger audience. And that changed everything.

In the days before home video, there were very few opportunities for a film to grow its audience after the initial theatrical release. The best you could hope for was to play revival houses. Or, if you were lucky, get a sale to television. *This Is Spinal Tap* flipped the old studio revenue model on its head. It became an early video-rental hit, with far greater success in the home-viewing market than it ever had in the theaters. As Harry puts it, "Before we knew it, we were the first non-porn production to make money in home video."

No demographic was more into the VHS version of *This Is Spinal Tap* than musicians. It became common, almost compulsory, for bands to watch and rewatch the movie on their tour buses. As Michael says, "We started hearing from every musician we met: 'The first things we get when we pull over the bus are ice, a few bottles of Jack Daniel's, and a copy of *Spinal Tap*.'"

As the Tap appreciation society grew, so, too, did requests for more Tap content. In 1990, Chris agreed to appear in character as Nigel at a major musicians' hangout, the Guitar Center in Hollywood. It was for the launch of Marshall's JCM900 amp. Marshall had specially outfitted their new signature amp with a volume knob that went *beyond* eleven, all the way up to twenty. In attendance were Peter Frampton, Dweezil Zappa, and Toto's Steve Lukather. Lukather is not only a great guitarist but a music-world connector, having worked with, among others, Paul McCartney, Ringo Starr, Michael Jackson, Eddie Van Halen, Randy Newman, Cher, and Jeff Beck.

"The thing about Chris when he's in character is that he won't break," Lukather says. "But I walked up to him at a moment when he wasn't surrounded by people and said, 'Hey, man, Steve Lukather, big fan.' He just kind of looked at me. But then I said, 'By the way, Jeff Beck thinks that what you're doing is fucking hilarious.' Chris broke character and said, 'He's not mad?'"

"Steve Lukather came up to me and said, 'Jeff Beck thinks the movie is cool. He wants to meet you,'" Chris recalls. "That was a weird thing to me—that people of that stature were liking it. Soon enough, Beck was in L.A. and he invited me to a session he was playing. He told me he's a fan; he thought the movie was funny. I gave him the leather jacket I wore in the film. A few days later, when he was leaving town, he called me and said, 'I left something for you.' I drove to A&M Studios in Hollywood. They were holding for me one of Beck's custom-designed guitars he did for Stratocaster: a Strat in sea-foam green. I took it home and called Jeff. I said, 'I can't believe you left me a guitar.' He said, 'What do you mean? I left you *two* guitars.' Someone had nicked one."

The key moment of the Guitar Center event happened right at the beginning, when a stretch limo arrived in front of the store. The first person to get out of the car was the Lord of Loud himself, Jim Marshall, the venerable English founder of Marshall Amplification. He was greeted with a polite smattering of applause. Then, out came Nigel, chomping on his gum and wearing his leather jacket over a leopard-print shirt. The crowd went wild. They broke into applause, with chants of "NI-gel! NI-gel!"

This, along with Jeff Beck's seal of approval, signaled to Chris, Michael, and Harry that, even six years after the movie's theatrical release, if the right opportunity presented itself, they might have to consider squeezing themselves back into their spandex pants and playing again.

CHAPTER 13

# 'Twas the Ultimate Mutation

In developing *This Is Spinal Tap*, we carefully constructed Tap's own reality and consciously kept the real world at bay. "We had a pretty strict policy on that," says Chris. "Even Nigel's favorite guitarist wasn't a real person, but a made-up bluesman named Blind Bubba Cheeks."

But as the cult of Tap grew, it became harder and harder to maintain this separation. As Harry puts it, "The real world dragged us into the real world." If the Hear 'n Aid single in 1985 seemed like a one-off trip into rock reality, by the early 1990s, it was evident that a lot of people in the music business wanted a piece of our loud, hapless fictitious band. In mid-1991, Harry, Chris, and Michael were invited by MTV to present, in character, the award for Best Metal/Hard Rock Video at that year's Video Music Awards. Aerosmith won for "The Other Side," which brought the boys face-to-face with Steven Tyler, the man who had stated that our movie bummed him out.

It was clear that Tap-mania, if you could call it that, was expanding rather than contracting. So, as the saying goes, you might as well lean into it. The guys decided to see where else they could take their characters. "We had already started writing songs and pitching them to each other, mixing demos and doing things like that," says Michael. At the VMAs, when David, Nigel, and Derek announced that Spinal Tap had re-formed, with plans for a new album and some live dates, the audience erupted into applause.

"We were starting to be presented with opportunities to do other things as Spinal Tap," says Chris. "We all had other things going on, but there were certain intervals in our lives when we had the time and we thought it would be fun to play. How could we say no? Who gets to do that?"

Adds Harry, "One of the reasons we came back to it, and that we keep coming back to it, is that we really enjoy playing together. And people want to see us play together. And it's not our full-time job, so we don't get tired of it."

That same year, work began on the second Spinal Tap album, *Break Like the Wind*. To herald its pending arrival, the band placed an ad in *Billboard* that read:

**DRUMMER DIED,**

**need new one.**

**Must have no**

**immediate family.**

The auditions were held on Halloween at the Los Angeles Coliseum. In character, the guys explained to a scrum of reporters what they were looking for.

NIGEL: The prime requisite would be, uh, good health.

**DAVID:** Survivability. Strong heartbeat. Good blood pressure.

**NIGEL:** Low cholesterol.

**DAVID:** That sort of thing.

**NIGEL:** With an optimistic outlook on life, knowing that you'll be dead soon.

A few hundred real aspirants showed up. The guys also roped in a few ringers: Mick Fleetwood of Fleetwood Mac, Micky Dolenz of the Monkees, Debbi Peterson of the Bangles, Gina Schock of the Go-Go's, and Stephen Perkins of the notoriously hard-living band Jane's Addiction. "I'm not really afraid of death, actually," Perkins told the press. "I've lived with the Jane's Addiction fellas for years now."

In reality, the "drummer auditions" were just a PR play. Ric Parnell was already on board as the drummer, returning as the late Mick Shrimpton's twin brother, Ric Shrimpton. Tap also had a new guy on keyboards. He was a young synthesizer prodigy who had come highly recommended by our first drummer, Russ Kunkel. His name was CJ Vanston, and he has been Tap's keyboardist ever since. CJ's actual name is Jeff Vanston. When he was still in his teens, CJ was the only white member of an R&B group that had two other Jeffs in it. To distinguish between them, they became AJ, BJ, and CJ—the first nickname was a tribute to the four-time Indy 500 winner A. J. Foyt; the second, BJ, stood for Black Jeff; and the third, CJ, stood for Caucasian Jeff, which is CJ's official Tap name, both on tour and in the film's sequel.

The new album, *Break Like the Wind*, included the first full-length version of the first song Nigel and David ever wrote, "All the Way Home," as well as the first recorded version of the flip side of "(Listen to the) Flower People," "Rainy Day Sun." The album also featured the soon-to-be classics "Bitch School" and "The Majesty of Rock."

The press release put out in advance of the album's launch included this passage:

> The album's first single, "Bitch School," has already caused some controversy among some militant women's groups, even before its official release. Tufnel explains, "We've heard that people have commented that 'Bitch School' is sexist. But basically, if you listen, you'll hear what it really is. It's about dogs—about training dogs! The three of us love dogs. Read the lyrics—'You're so fetching when you are down on all fours.' How can you misconstrue that?"

For *Break Like the Wind*'s enigmatic title song ("We are the footprints across the sands / We are the thumbs on a stranger's hands"), Steve Lukather, who produced the track, lined up a murderers' row of guitar soloists: Joe Satriani, Slash, Jeff Beck, Lukather himself, and, of course, Nigel Tufnel. Says Lukather, "The comedy of it was that everyone got eight bars and each solo went up half a step, so that by the time Jeff went at the end, it was way high. Slash insisted on recording his solo at a blisteringly insane decibel level. It was amazing, but he was playing so loud that he didn't realize he was in the wrong key. Which was such a Spinal Tap thing to do. But I had him redo the solo in the correct key and it was perfect."

Harry contributed a song called "Just Begin Again," written in the maudlin "power ballad" format popular at the time on hard-rock radio. Lukather produced that one as well. The guys thought it would work perfectly as David St. Hubbins's grab for soulful gravitas.

"It was the heyday of the duet," says Michael. "Natalie Cole singing 'Unforgettable' with her dead father, Frank Sinatra's *Duets* album, and, most egregiously, Kenny G overlaying his sax on Louis Armstrong's recording of 'What a Wonderful World,' which resulted in an extraordinary screed from Pat Metheny. He condemned Kenny G for 'musical necrophilia.'

"We had been talking about doing a duet on the album, and 'Just Begin Again' seemed to fit the bill. Steve Lukather was working on a project with Cher and said, 'What about Cher?' She agreed to do it, somewhat reluctantly. I think her son Elijah Blue was a fan of ours. She put down her vocal separately. I never met her and still haven't. We asked her to film a video of herself singing for when we played the song on tour, but she didn't want to do that. So we just used a photo of her and superimposed a moving mouth over it, like the old *Clutch Cargo* cartoon."

These high-profile guest appearances marked a crossing of the Rubicon. Spinal Tap had slipped into the real world. In 1992, the band booked a spring-summer "shed tour" of big outdoor venues. As a warm-up, they jumped into the deep end, performing before an audience of 72,000 at Wembley Stadium as a featured act in the Freddie Mercury Tribute Concert for AIDS Awareness. Tap found themselves on a bill that included not only the surviving members of Queen, but David Bowie, Annie Lennox, George Michael, Elton John, Metallica, Guns N' Roses, and Def Leppard. Tap's parallel universe was being subsumed by the actual universe. And this was no black-hole type of thing. They were sharing a stage with real rock icons.

The band's appearance at the Mercury tribute started off well. A team of sexy young women in shorty beefeater costumes rolled out a red carpet that led to the stage. The guys strode out in crowns and ermine-trimmed coronation robes. After the beefeaterettes stripped them of their regalia, Tap was set to launch into a fist-pumping rendition of "The Majesty of Rock." But fate held other ideas—and they came in the form of a classic Spinal Tap moment.

"There was no sound coming out of my amp," recalls Chris. "It wasn't working. So we had this long, really scary delay. The crew was slow to move on the issue because they thought we were doing some kind of bit. We weren't. Harry and Michael had to work the crowd for over three minutes. It felt like two years. They ended up rewiring my guitar through a different amp that had none of my effects. So I was basically lost. There were times where I just stopped because I didn't even know where I was."

Fortunately, the rest of the tour went smoothly. The reaction was so positive that it was sort of confusing. "Playing these bigger venues, with thousands of people showing up, it didn't always make sense to me," says Chris. "Why are they here? Why are they cheering so hard? I think in some cases, they felt like they were in the movie."

"In a sense," says Michael, "we were pretending to be a real band and they were pretending to be our real fans."

"Except you wonder if it had been taken to the next level," counters Chris. "There was one gig where we walked backstage and there were half-naked women sitting in the dressing room. Actual groupies. You think, 'Do they know? Do they think we're a real band? Do they think this is what we really look like?'"

"I think some people show up at a venue not wondering about satirical content," concludes Michael. "They're just thinking, 'This looks like a party.'"

**L**et it be known for the record that Chris, Michael, and Harry did not engage in naughty extracurricular activities. And their contract rider, unlike Van Halen's, demanded little more than decent wine, good chocolate, and fresh fruit. It was a fruit platter, oddly enough, that led to the band's closest brush with rock 'n' roll depravity. This was in Mansfield, Massachusetts, in the dressing room of the Great Woods Center for the Performing Arts.

"There was a table with a bunch of grapes," Chris recalls. "I picked up a green grape. And Michael was in the process of getting dressed, wearing nothing but a jockstrap."

"You know what the back of a jockstrap is like? There is none," says Michael. "So I was facing the mirror, about to change my shirt or whatever. I heard Chris say, 'Mike, hold still.' I looked up and saw that he was going to hit me in the ass with this grape. So he threw the grape. And without using my hands or turning around, I caught it. The word that came to my mind was 'prehensile.'"

With Michael still flexing his grip, Chris took a photo for posterity.

This important event has come to be known within our ranks as the Grape Incident, or the Grapes of Heinie.

**T**he crowning achievement of Tap's 1992 appearances was their concert at London's Royal Albert Hall, the prestigious Victorian venue where Dylan, the Beatles, the Who, and Pink Floyd had played. NBC commemorated the event with a special called *The Return of Spinal Tap*, hosted by the former MTV veejay Martha Quinn.

In catch-up segments with the band, we learned that David had been running a soccer clinic for girls in Pomona, California. Nigel had taken to inventing things and came up with a wineglass whose sides folded up for easy storage in a picnic basket. Unfortunately, he hadn't allowed for the possibility of leakage, of which there was a great deal. Derek had returned to his native Nilford, England, to help his elderly father, Duff Smalls, with his telephone-sanitizing business, SaniFone. There was footage of David and Nigel returning to their old neighborhood of Squatney and discovering that their favored pub, the Queen's Lips, was now called the Gun, and that their first studio was now a weed-infested vacant lot.

We also caught up with Marty DiBergi, who occupied a temporary workspace in the hallway of an office building. Marty justified the location for its proximity to the men's room and a pay phone. He acknowledged that the band bore a grudge against him for *This Is Spinal Tap*, and that his follow-up film, *Kramer vs. Kramer vs. Godzilla*, had underperformed at the box office.

In the concert footage, Nigel and Derek beatboxed while David performed a hip-hop version of "Sex Farm." "Stonehenge" was once again undermined—this time because the Stonehenge replica was too *big* to get into the venue. A video screen above the band showed the roadies struggling to jam the oversized monument through the loading bay.

"In every subsequent era of doing 'Stonehenge,' we've done the joke a different way," says Chris. "For Royal Albert Hall, it was too big to get in. In another venue, it was just a FedEx guy coming out with an envelope containing a tiny reproduction. When we played Wembley Arena, we had an inflatable Stonehenge that went flaccid as the air went out of it. It smothered the dancing Druids."

The performance at the Royal Albert Hall also holds the distinction of being the catalyst for another Tap-induced romance. A couple of days before the concert, Harry, Chris, and one of the Stonehenge dwarves were hanging out in the lobby of the Chelsea Harbour Hotel. Waiting to check in, Harry heard some beautiful music coming from another part of the hotel. The three guys followed the sound to the lounge, where a singer named Judith Owen was performing. As Chris recalls, Harry took one look at Ms. Owen and his eyes bugged out of his head like a cartoon character's.

Judith, it turned out, had recognized Harry—she was a Tap fan and knew that he was Derek. After she finished her set, Harry chatted up Judith and invited her to the Royal Albert Hall show. Two days later, they went out on a date. Eight months after that, they got married. Harry and Judith have now been married for over thirty years. Once again, the Tap cupid hit the bull's-eye.

Since they were now an actual touring band, Spinal Tap took on a manager—not a hapless Ian Faith type, but a real and competent one named Harriet Sternberg. Besides overseeing the day-to-day operations of the band, Harriet fielded requests from corporate entities hot to capitalize on Tap's fame for their big ad campaigns.

Well, the word "big" might be a bit too generous—unless you consider an Australian company called Finder's that made microwavable stuffed pizza rolls called, yes, Rock 'n' Rolls big. Yet how could they turn this opportunity down? We open on the band backstage before a show.

    NIGEL, *poking his finger into a plain roll*: See, this is just an ordinary roll. Look: you can poke and poke, nobody's home!

But in these geezers [breaking open a Rock 'n' Roll], look! Look what's in Rock 'n' Rolls!

**DEREK,** *in curlers*: It's like a wedding between bread and filling.

The word "classic" comes to mind.

In advance of the 1996 Summer Olympics in Atlanta, a more prestigious suitor came calling. IBM was one of the Games' chief sponsors and a major coordinator of its technical operations. The company's head of advertising told the *New York Times*, "We wanted to reach out further to a younger generation of decision-makers with whom it's important to enhance the relevance of the IBM brand. Spinal Tap offers an engaging, fun way of telling the story of what we'll do at the Games."

Speaking on behalf of the band, Harriet Sternberg explained that IBM was a "very close second" on Tap's list of preferred sponsorship partners, the first being the adult-diaper brand Depends.

In the IBM ad, while Nigel plays a guitar solo, the guys are shown onstage talking to each other under their breath.

**DAVID:** You know, Derek, our third comeback tour could become a logistical nightmare. We've got nutritionists, au pairs, personal trainers . . .

**DEREK:** Not to mention the erupting-volcano apparatus.

**NIGEL:** Let's bring in IBM!

Alas, the '96 Olympics turned out not to be IBM's finest hour. "IBM was bragging in the commercial about how they were responsible for all of the tech stuff at the Atlanta Olympics," says Harry.

"The Spinal Tap upshot was that there was a terrible raft of failures of the tech stuff."

First of all, the IBM-designed website for the Olympic Games proved buggy and slow. Then the company's brand-new "Info '96" system to provide competition results to news organizations failed, forcing the Olympics staff to send results to the media the old-fashioned way, by using human runners carrying pieces of paper. Nine years later, IBM, a pioneer in personal computing, sold off its entire PC division to the Chinese tech giant Lenovo. Ian Faith couldn't have mismanaged things any better.

CHAPTER 14

# All the Way Home

After the IBM triumph/fiasco, Spinal Tap entered a five-year period of dormancy. Then, in 2001, a theatrical rerelease of *This Is Spinal Tap* sparked a mini-tour. Tap played the Greek Theatre in Los Angeles, the House of Blues in Las Vegas, and, as Derek referred to it onstage, *Carnegie fucking Hall*. And due to popular demand, the band added a second New York show, at the Beacon Theatre.

For these dates, Tap's opening act was the Folksmen, a Kingston Trio–like group made up of Chris, Harry, and Michael as their folkie alter egos, Alan Barrows (Chris on mandolin, banjo, guitar, and vocals), Jerry Palter (Michael on guitar and vocals), and Mark Shubb (Harry on upright bass and vocals). The Folksmen were not brand-new characters, having made their first public appearance in 1984 in an *SNL* episode hosted by Michael. But they were not yet widely known. Spinal Tap's 2001 tour took place two years before the release of Chris's film *A Mighty Wind*, which would introduce the Folksmen to a sizable moviegoing audience. So, before that, many of the people in Tap's audiences didn't realize that Alan, Jerry, and Mark were played by the same guys who played Nigel, David, and Derek—and damn it, they hadn't paid good money to see three old men sing about steam-engine trains and the Spanish Civil War. They wanted Tap. As such, the Folksmen's set was often interrupted by impatient chants of "Tap! Tap! Tap!"

A lot had changed since the guys had last toured as Tap. Says Harry, "We were rehearsing and somebody said to us, 'The joke band is the only one that's playing live.' Because by that point, nearly everyone was singing to tracks."

Spinal Tap has never sung or played to prerecorded tracks, and it remains a source of exasperation to the guys that people are still surprised by their musical proficiency. "Even at Carnegie Hall," says Chris, "a writer came up to me after the show and said, 'Were you guys really playing?' We *still* get that: 'I didn't realize you guys can actually play.' The thing about our situation is, people can't reconcile the idea of being able to do both comedy and music. That can't be a thing. The music has to be not real because we're funny people making fun of things."

"The irony," says Harry, "is that so many people in previous generations of comedy were good musicians. Jack Benny was a really good violinist. Victor Borge was an accomplished pianist. Henny Youngman was a violinist. Morey Amsterdam played the cello. As opposed to when we put together our shows, which run to almost two hours, there are no inherent jokes or sketches. We're playing as a band. It's a different thing."

In 2002, I was notified that the National Film Registry, which is administered by the Library of Congress, had added *This Is Spinal Tap* to its collection of "culturally, historically, or aesthetically significant films" made in America. The Registry did not specify which boxes of significance we checked, but we were thrilled. I mean, we were now on a list of films that included *Citizen Kane*, *Casablanca*, *On the Waterfront*, and *Lawrence of Arabia*. I'm going to go out on a limb and say that we got more laughs than all those films combined.

A spokesman for the National Film Preservation Board praised our movie as "very deft" and went on to make this peculiar observation: "The phrase 'Spinal Tap' has almost become synonymous for something that isn't as it appears to be. I've heard it used in politics. Legislation that isn't what it seems to be is called a Spinal Tap."

I myself have never heard the words "Spinal Tap" used in this manner. "These go to eleven" and "a fine line between stupid and clever," yes, but not this. Whatever. We were sincerely, unironically flattered that our low-budget film had earned such status.

That same year, the *Shorter Oxford English Dictionary*, as the abridged, two-volume version of that reference book is known, added the phrase "(up) to eleven" and defined its meaning as "up to maximum volume." Sixteen years later, in 2018, popular usage of "(up) to eleven" had become ubiquitous and ever more liberally interpreted. Volkswagen used the words "This one goes to eleven" to promote its Turbo Beetle. A California vintner released a line of premium "Eleven" wines. This all warranted a more expansive definition in the longer-form version of the *Oxford English Dictionary*, which reads:

colloquial (usually humorous) *(up) to eleven: so as to reach or surpass the maximum level or limit; to an extreme or intense degree. Esp in to turn (something) up to eleven and variants.*

*[With allusion to a scene in the rock-music mockumentary* This Is Spinal Tap *(1984), featuring an amplifier with control knobs having 11 rather than 10 as the highest setting]*

Per Fiona McPherson, a senior editor at the *OED*:

We maintain a watch list of candidate words and phrases for addition to the *OED*, which includes suggestions from editors and readers as well as targeted reading programs and wider tracking and analysis of language change. This allows us to monitor the suggestions and identify those words which have already gathered sufficient evidence to be considered for inclusion, while keeping the door open for those that aren't quite there yet.

In the case of "(up) to eleven," this was suggested by an editor. While it remains synonymous with *This Is Spinal Tap*, our research found it in a variety of different contexts referring to anything which can surpass the (seemingly) maximum level, or, dare I say, go "one louder." The selection of quotations that we have in the entry range from exercise to economics. It was this broadening usage into non-musical contexts that was a major factor in it being included, demonstrating that it is now more than just a much-loved quotation from the film and has well and truly entered the language.

So not only did Spinal Tap play Carnegie fucking Hall. Now the band was in the *Oxford fucking English Dictionary*.

The film is also cited in the dictionary's definition of the word "rockumentary." The infiltration of *This Is Spinal Tap* into culture and popular discourse is mind-boggling, even to us. In 2006, American Express licensed "Gimme Some Money" for use in a commercial for its SimplyCash business card. The title *Smell the Glove* has been appropriated by at least a dozen microbreweries as the name of a craft beer. The phrase "Spinal Tap moment" is so entrenched in the rock lexicon as a term for any incident involving band misfortune, equipment malfunctions, or public humiliation that NPR, *Guitar World*, and *Ultimate Classic Rock* have all run features in which real-life rockers describe their Spinal Tap moments.

As I learned firsthand from Max Bernstein, the son of my late friend Nora Ephron, who wrote the screenplay for *When Harry Met Sally*, Tap's appeal has spanned generations. When Max was barely into his teens, he saw Tap at the Beacon Theatre during the *Break Like the Wind* tour and became a fan. Now a successful rock guitarist, Max has toured with Taylor Swift, Miley Cyrus, and Ke$ha. At a gathering to celebrate his stepfather Nick Pileggi's ninetieth birthday, Max pulled down his shirt and revealed to me, on the back of his left shoulder, a tattoo that was a perfect depiction of the graphic on the cover of *Shark Sandwich*.

Even my USS OORAL SEA baseball cap has become a totem of sorts. In 1986, my good friend Bobby Colomby, the drummer for Blood, Sweat & Tears, suggested his friend Mark Knopfler of Dire Straits to compose the music for *The Princess Bride*. Mark said he would do it, but only on one condition: that Marty's cap appear somewhere in the movie. I told him I didn't think it would fit it into a period film set in a mythical land of swashbucklers. Then I realized that I could place the cap in the framing scenes, where Peter Falk reads the book version of *The Princess Bride* to his grandson. So, if you look closely, you can see the USS OORAL SEA cap hanging on a lamp in the grandson's bedroom.

Somewhere, and I really hope I'm wrong about this, there might be a film student at some $80,000-a-year liberal arts college majoring in Spinal Tap.

In 2007, I was approached by Kevin Wall, a man who had considerable experience organizing benefit concerts. He was putting together an event with Al Gore called Live Earth. It was to be a series of megaconcerts around the globe whose proceeds would be dedicated to initiatives to fight climate change.

Kevin wanted Tap for the London concert, whose bill also included Metallica, Madonna, the Beastie Boys, the Foo Fighters, and the Red Hot Chili Peppers. The guys said yes, so it was back to Wembley Stadium, this time with Tap friend and fan Ricky Gervais introducing me as Marty, and Marty introducing the band. Caucasian Jeff returned on keyboards, bringing with him a new drummer, Skippy Skuffleton, the Tap stage name of Gregg Bissonette, the touring drummer in Ringo Starr's All-Starr Band. Apropos of the event, Tap surprised the crowd with a newfound political consciousness and unveiled an eco-anthem titled "Warmer Than Hell," in which even Satan finds Earth too hot:

*Beelzebub's in Brighton*
*The last time there he froze*

*Now he says the sand is far too hot*
*For his poor cloven toes*

The highlight of Tap's Live Earth set, and possibly of the whole event, was an epic version of "Big Bottom" featuring a total of nineteen bassists, among them Rob Trujillo of Metallica, Nate Mendel of the Foo Fighters, and Adam Yauch of the Beastie Boys.

Live Earth whetted the guys' appetite for another album and tour. In the summer of 2009, Tap's third album, *Back from the Dead*, was released. It featured "Warmer Than Hell" and "Short and Sweet," as well as—finally—a full version of "Jazz Odyssey," now spelled "Jazz Oddyssey" and broken into three separate movements.

As in 1992, the plan was to do a series of dates in outdoor sheds. But just as the tour arrangements were falling into place, the 2008 economic crash happened. Says Harry, "All of the sponsors that had been tentatively lined up for a Spinal Tap tour failed. So the choice was either to quit or to go out in stripped-down form, with minimal expenses."

Out of these pinched circumstances was born a series of acoustic dates, 2009's Unwigged & Unplugged tour. Because the guys were not in costume, they were freed up to play not only Tap songs but ones they had composed for *A Mighty Wind* and for *Red, White, and Blaine*, the fictitious musical staged by the citizens of Blaine, Missouri, in Chris's classic film *Waiting for Guffman*. (If you weren't aware that "Stool Boom" and "Nothing Ever Happens on Mars" are Guest-Shearer compositions, now you are.)

But the wigged-and-plugged-in Spinal Tap was not done. There were two last hurrahs for the band that year, both fittingly in their "native" England. First, they played the Pyramid Stage of the country's biggest summer festival, Glastonbury, to a crowd of more than 100,000 people. Then, four days later, they headlined at the 12,500-seat Wembley Arena. At Glastonbury, the crowd had the privilege of being serenaded with the band's festival-specific anthem, "Stinkin' Up the Great Outdoors":

> *Late afternoon in the open air*
> *A human sea made out of mud and hair*
> *Ain't nothing like a festival crowd*
> *There's too many people so we play too loud*
>
> *Touch down, the plane's on the ground*
> *Look for the drummer and he's nowhere around*
> *We're running late*
> *At least an hour*
> *No time to rest*
> *No time to shower*
> *Now we're stinkin' up the great outdoors*

In front of an audience of this size, the distinction between a satirical band and real band was academic. "It was one of those moments where, as a player, you're not thinking about being in a fake band," says Chris. "It was *fun*, looking out at the crowd. It was hard to even imagine how big it was until we saw the BBC footage later, the crane shot over the whole site. You just think, 'Holy fuck!'"

For their last live performance of "Big Bottom," the guys were joined by Jarvis Cocker of Pulp on bass. A parade of local women filed out to strut their stuff onstage. A fan in the audience held aloft a homemade banner that read SPANIEL TAP. Perfect.

### INTERLUDE

# I Look to the Stars and the Answer Is Clear

Upon its initial release, *This Is Spinal Tap* resonated with rock musicians and has continued to do so ever since. Here, some stars recount the effect the film had on them and their own "Spinal Tap moments."

## Slash, Guns N' Roses

I saw the movie when it came out in 1984. At the time, it was just a funny movie. I hadn't joined Guns N' Roses yet; I was just in garage bands and whatnot. It wasn't until we'd been touring for a while that I started to realize how much of the stuff in the movie was stuff I was going through on a regular basis. It was so painfully real.

Around the middle of 1988, we crested this wave and the band suddenly got really big because of "Sweet Child O' Mine." We were still an opening band, though, touring with Aerosmith. But now we were filling the buildings before they went on. When we came home, we did a one-off show in Texas Stadium as part of a festival. We thought we had all this touring experience, so we didn't show up for sound check: "We'll just walk out and we'll be fine."

It was one of the worst shows that we ever played. The band just utterly fell apart onstage. None of us could hear each other. And it was raining. Then the tour ended and I was back in my apartment in L.A. One day, I was opening up the mail, and in one envelope was an *Appetite for Destruction* cassette broken in half. The letter that came with it said, "We saw you at Texas Stadium and it was the worst thing we ever saw." This fan was so disappointed that he sent us our album back!

A funny story about Axl, my partner in crime: Way after the movie came out, I had some knobs made that went to eleven, as a joke. He thought they were real.

## Chris Frantz & Tina Weymouth, Talking Heads

TINA: We saw the movie for the first time right after we finished our last tour, the one captured in *Stop Making Sense*.

CHRIS: We were just like, "Oh, my God."

TINA: Just floored by the genius of it and also happy that we had insisted to Jonathan Demme that in our film, we would have no interviews with the band, no backstage footage, no following us around.

CHRIS: We had a certain degree of prescience, because at that time, we hadn't yet seen *This Is Spinal Tap*. But if we'd had all those things, our movie would have been more like *This Is Spinal Tap*. That said, I do remember sitting in hotel lobbies and having big, more successful bands blow us off because they had to go wait for the limo.

**TINA:** We were driving a station wagon.

**CHRIS:** I once lost my cool like Nigel before a show in Philadelphia. The caterer brought in a deli platter in a garbage bag, and he didn't discreetly remove the garbage bag before he came into our dressing room. He just set the platter on the counter, still in the bag. I yelled, "Get that garbage bag out of here!"

**TINA:** Oh, Chris. I did not know you had this issue.

## Don Henley, the Eagles

I just rewatched the film. I laughed, but it's also very triggering for me. We had infighting from the very beginning and then it continued through all the different members. When Michael McKean says, "There have been thirty-seven people in this band," it's funny and true to life.

We got lost backstage, too. Our first road manager was the janitor from the Troubadour. We would drive around in a station wagon and couldn't even find the building, let alone the stage. And the whole thing of getting to the hotel desk and hearing that they don't have the rooms—that happened to us numerous times. Our road manager, just like Ian Faith, would get in a fight with the desk clerk. We usually had to find another place to stay.

In the early seventies we had some pretty disastrous bookings, too. We had a gig outdoors in Sweden with snow on the ground, fucking freezing. Our manager, Irving Azoff, was in the wings, standing by a heater with his hands in his pockets. Glenn Frey yelled at Irving, "Get away from the heater! You're gonna have to suffer through this just like we are."

When Nigel says, "We're closer than brothers and brothers always fight"—I've said those exact words regarding Glenn and me. We were on the same side most of the time, but it changes over time. In the beginning, when you're young, you have the same mission. You can sit in the same room with acoustic guitars and pianos and write together. But as time goes by, you find yourself writing remotely, just sending your stuff over to the other guy.

When David and Derek are at the end of the tour, that sad scene on the Hyatt rooftop where they're talking about doing their musical about Jack the Ripper, *Saucy Jack*—we always talked about *Hotel California: The Musical*. Glenn was working on it when he died. I think he took some of the songs to the drama department at the University of Michigan to have some of the kids there play around with it.

But being a drummer who is alive is in itself a victory. I haven't exploded.

## Steve Lukather & Steve Porcaro, Toto

**STEVE L:** We were working on the soundtrack for *Dune* in '84 when somebody told us, "You guys really need to see this film." All six of us went together to a matinee in Westwood. There were only four other people in the theater. We were dying with laughter. The other people kept turning around and looking at us, like, "Why are you laughing?" We understood where it all was coming from.

**STEVE P:** In 1982, when we were on tour for *Toto IV*, the album that has "Rosanna" and "Africa" on it, we commissioned this stage prop, a reproduction of the sword emblem on the album's cover. But we literally never laid eyes upon it until it was lowered from the ceiling while we were playing live onstage at Budokan. Unlike a sword, it was made of some kind of flimsy, lightweight material, so it was just wobbling and twisting in the breeze, which was embarrassing. Soon it was spinning off-axis to a point where it was comical.

**STEVE L:** It looked like a papier-mâché high school project. It was just like the napkin bit with "Stonehenge," but the Tap movie was not even out yet!

## Aimee Mann

I saw the movie with my band 'Til Tuesday, when it came out in 1984, right before we went on tour with Hall & Oates. The playing we had done to that point was just in New England: drive up, do a sound check, go get something to eat, sit backstage, play the show, and then drive home that night.

When we saw *This Is Spinal Tap* for the first time, it was like "Hardy-har-har. This is all so hilarious. Nigel making a big deal about the flat meat and the tiny little bread. The band doing the in-store and nobody's there. Oh, this is so hilarious and exaggerated and comedy gold."

Then we went out on tour. Within a couple of weeks, we were saying, "That movie is not a comedy. It's a fucking documentary." Especially the backstage rider. Because when you're only driving from Boston to Beverly, Mass., either eating after the sound check or late at night when you get home, you're not dependent on what's backstage. The idea of a rider just seems so self-important. Why would you even need a rider?

On tour with Hall & Oates, we realized: "Because this could literally be the one meal I get all day. I can't leave the venue when people are already lined up." So on subsequent viewings, when I saw the scene with Nigel with the food, I was like, "I'm on his fucking side. Give him a full piece of bread! Let him have the dignity of an actual sandwich!"

*Spinal Tap* covered every dumb, irritating aspect of touring. At the old City Winery in New York, the dressing room was literally on the stage. So you couldn't leave the dressing room to use the bathroom without crossing the stage. And near the end of the movie, when David and Derek say, "We should write a musical," I was like, "Yes! That's a great idea." When you're putting out records and touring, there's a hamster-wheel feel to it. You start to think, "I'd like to be musically creative in a different direction." And now I'm working on a couple of musicals.

## Rosanne Cash

I went to see *This Is Spinal Tap* in the theater when it came out. I'd been touring since 1978 and I was *dying*, identifying moments of the film that I'd experienced. Getting lost in the tunnels of the backstage area? Yes, a million times, that's happened! Once, I found myself left behind by the guys—and I say *guys*, literally, because I never toured with women until fairly recently—and I was lost in this empty labyrinth. I found an elevator and got in. A woman appeared out of nowhere who had been stalking me. She got in the elevator with me. The door closed and she got really close to me. I got off the elevator as quick as I could, found my tour manager, and I said, "You guys fucking *left* me!"

My equivalent of opening for a puppet show came in Germany.

I made my first album in Munich, for a German label called Ariola Records. I went back there to promote it. A gentleman at Ariola Records said, "We have this big opportunity for you in Bavaria. There's going to be thirty thousand people, and it's going to be at noon. In a tent."

I said, "A tent in the countryside?"

He said, "Yes, absolutely. And it's going to be broadcast on the radio."

So we went there. As we pulled in, I saw that it was a circus tent. From the entrance I was supposed to go into, a giraffe walked out. There were more animals milling around inside. And there was a stage and an audience of maybe fifty people. Under the big top.

It turned out that, yes, my performance was going to be on the radio, but they asked me to lip-sync. I said, "Lip-syncing on the radio? That's the same as just playing the record." The guy said, "Yes, yes, yes, and we're so excited for you to do this!" So I went onstage, one hundred percent humiliated. They played the record while I pretended to sing. And while this was going on, the circus animals were on the stage, moving all around me.

## Rob Halford & Ian Hill, Judas Priest

ROB: When the movie came out, Glenn Tipton, our guitar player, and I snuck into a matinee screening in San Diego. It wasn't particularly busy. Within minutes, Glenn and I were roaring, because we thought, "This is us. This is Priest." But there were some metalheads in the theater who didn't appreciate that it was satire. They were going, "What the fuck is this shit, man? I thought this was going to be about a *real* band. I want my money back."

The plotline about drummers blowing up? That kind of actually happened. Dave Holland, rest his soul, was our drummer, and he had an incident like that.

**IAN:** People used to throw firecrackers onto the stage, aiming at him. It pissed him off because he was a stationary target.

**ROB:** Dave had Perspex soundproofing around him, which also served as protection. But some kid managed to throw an M-80 over the shield. It landed in the hole of the kick drum and blew it up. Dave tried to keep playing through the smoke and fire. He didn't get hurt, but his plan to protect himself was a miserable failure.

On the *Defenders of the Faith* tour in 1984, we put Dave on a huge drum riser that was twenty feet in the air. We never told him. So he came out onstage and was like, "I can't go up there. It's too high." We convinced him he was safe. But a band's members need to keep in eye contact with each other, you know? Which was impossible for Dave when we were all at the front of the stage. So we had to turn around and wave our arms at him, like semaphore.

We recently lost our original drummer, John Hinch—another one, rest his soul. He was a lovely guy from a posh background. We've got more drummers in heaven than on the road.

**IAN:** On a different tour, I think for *British Steel*, we were traveling through Texas when our tour bus broke down in the desert. We had a show to get to in San Antonio. I don't know how the hell he did it, but our tour manager managed to arrange for a helicopter, one of those big Huey things from the Vietnam War. But after it landed, it wouldn't start up again. They had to radio back to base for another helicopter to bring a new battery. Then a police helicopter arrived, wondering why there was a large helicopter by the side of the road. Then the other helicopter arrived with the battery. So there were now three helicopters.

They got the first helicopter going and we thought, "Okay, now our problems are over with." We flew to San Antonio. The plan was to land on the roof of the Hyatt, which had a heliport on top. But some other helicopter had beaten us to it. We were rerouted to the San Antonio airport, where they put us in a holding pattern, flying around in circles.

We were all looking at our watches. We had a show to play! So the pilot said, "I'll just land in the car park." When we did, we were immediately surrounded by all these border police with guns drawn. They thought we were smuggling Mexicans in.

**ROB:** We have a picture of us with the police guys. They were all saying to us, "You're breakin' the law, breakin' the law."

**IAN:** In the end, they let us go and we were only about ten minutes late to start the show.

To this day, whenever any of the four of us is approached by a musician who's eager to regale us with his or her "Tap stories," we continue to feel validated about everything we set out to do.

CHAPTER 15

# We'll Go Back in Time to That Mystic Land

We never made money from *This Is Spinal Tap*. Though Chris, Michael, and Harry were able to earn a bit through records, concerts, and ads, the actual movie, for all its quotability and National Film Registry status, earned us nada. Which is Spanish for *bupkis*. Which is Yiddish for "we got screwed."

And when I say we got nothing, I mean we got *nothing*. The deal we signed with Embassy Pictures had the four of us splitting 40 percent of the film's net profits. You'd think that this would amount to a decent amount of coin. But thanks to Hollywood's "creative accounting," we received literally pennies for our work. I'll explain.

*This Is Spinal Tap* has had a long and tortuous ownership history. Back in 1985, Norman Lear and Jerry Perenchio sold Embassy Pictures to the Coca-Cola Company, which at the time owned Columbia Pictures. Columbia then sold off Embassy to the Italian producer Dino De Laurentiis. Soon thereafter, his company went belly-up and its film assets were absorbed by a company called Paravision International, which was owned by the French cosmetics giant L'Oréal, from whom we never got so much as a tube of lip gloss.

Then, in 1994, Paravision's film assets were acquired by Studio-Canal, a film production and distribution company owned by the French conglomerate Vivendi SE. This made Vivendi the proud rights holder to *This Is Spinal Tap* and its related licensing. Now, stay with me if you can: between 1989 and 2006, Vivendi reported only $98 in income from the *Spinal Tap* soundtrack sales, and, between 1984 and 2006, a grand total of $81 in merchandising income.

The four of us have been fortunate to have had fulfilling careers, both creatively and financially. Chris and I direct films, Michael stars in plays and TV shows, and Harry is the man of a thousand voices on *The Simpsons*. So it's not as if we were desperate for money. But this just wasn't right. So Harry decided to do something about it. "It came to a point where I was well enough paid by *The Simpsons* to think, 'I can afford to do this,'" he says. "We had been stuck in this situation for so long. The film does some business every year. It's on TV in England all the time, on the Beeb. It does well in Australia. It does okay here in America. So the film company could just sit back and do nothing and collect the revenue that the movie generates every year. And that's all they did do—sit back. And when we went out on tour, we had to split our profits with the film company in some measure. I thought, 'Why are we paying splits, on our infrequent tours, to people who are doing nothing to promote the film?' That was one of my major motivations, apart from my ability to afford it, to initiate the lawsuit."

In 2016, Harry, acting on behalf of all four of us, filed suit against Vivendi SE, seeking punitive and compensatory damages, as well as the full rights to the film and its related content. Lawsuit-wise, it was convenient one-stop shopping, because at the time, the rights to the Spinal Tap albums were held by the Universal Music Group, in which Vivendi had an 80 percent stake. Nonetheless, Harry had to operate on two tracks.

"There was a day when I had meetings in Beverly Hills with representatives of both StudioCanal and Universal about rights," he recalls. "I went from one room, where the movie people were quite aggressive in their position, to another room, where the people from Universal Music were like, 'Well, let's make a deal.'"

It took four years and what Harry describes as "a byzantine tour of the legal system," but he finally reached a settlement with Vivendi and Universal. I'm not allowed to disclose the financial terms, but what I can say, with a tremendous debt of gratitude to Harry, is that as a result of his efforts, the four of us now own all existing and future intellectual property rights to *This Is Spinal Tap* and any and all related products: the songs, the merch, sequels, and any and all Tap-related tchotchkes, which is Yiddish for tchotchkes.

It took nearly an additional two years for the specifics of the settlement to be worked out. When we met to sign the appropriate documents, it marked the first time in a long while that all four of us were in the same room. We talked about what we might do now that we had the rights.

Since the film first came out, I can't tell you how many times we've all been asked about doing a sequel. We never even considered it. Why fuck with a classic?

But as the fortieth anniversary of the release of *This Is Spinal Tap* approached, we began to entertain the previously heretical idea of doing a sequel. We got together at my house to kick around ideas. At first, there was resistance to the thought of even "going there." The bar was too high, and, as we looked at each other, we noticed something inescapable: we were old. Could the cumulative three hundred years of the four of us get our schnadling chops up again?

"The widespread later acceptance of the first film, along with the honor of being in the National Film Registry, only served to underscore the idea of *I think we've done it. Why do it again?*" says Harry.

Adds Chris, "I had a lot of concerns. First, is this even a thing? Could we come up with an idea good enough to justify a movie? And then, how do we deal with age? Prior to making the movie, I watched a lot of rock documentaries. It's hard to miss the look of eighty-year-old guys who were first playing together fifty or sixty years ago. Look at Keith Richards's face. Or Robert Plant. I saw a picture of him that accompanied some recent interview and it almost looks like some special effects person said, 'Can I go crazy here?' It's a very stark reality, visually. And when you look at our faces, you realize, 'Oh. That's us, too.' Especially when you compare us to how we look in the first movie. We were in our thirties, but to me, we all look twenty-five, even younger than we actually were."

But after a few more meetings, we saw that we still made each other laugh. "Basically," says Michael, "what we'd do is get together for three hours and talk about Jimmy Durante, or 'Boy, wasn't that Sid Melton something?' You know, really connecting with the youth market. Some days we didn't have any ideas and our conversations had nothing to do with the film. But we were having fun."

Once we finally crossed the threshold into "I guess we're doing this," we started working up a storyline. We went about it the same way we did for *This Is Spinal Tap*. For a time, we met for brainstorming sessions at an office lent to us by the film producer Frank Marshall. While there, we learned that Simon Fuller, the British producer and entrepreneur behind the TV shows *Pop Idol* and *American Idol*, wanted to meet us.

Fuller, who is also the driving force behind *ABBA Voyage*, a London show in which hologram avatars of the Swedish pop group's four members (known as ABBAtars) play before a live audience, told us he had some ideas he wanted to share with us. No, the guys will not be sending a group of TAPatars out on tour. But Simon did inspire us to create a new character, a confident British showman who is enlisted to promote Tap's reunion concert. Unlike Simon Fuller, our guy is clinically incapable of enjoying music.

As a story started to emerge, we moved the operation to Harry's house in Santa Monica, where we set up two bulletin boards. Michael printed up a new set of Grimsbies, and I started tacking up scene ideas for *Tap II*.

Tony Hendra, who played Ian Faith, passed away in 2021. This led us to the idea that Ian's adult daughter had inherited her father's managerial contract, which called for one final Tap concert. We played around with the name for Ian's daughter. Faith Faith was a bit cutesy. Charity Faith was a stretch. We settled on Hope Faith—a Goldilocks "just right" choice.

In the fiction of our story, Hope initially believes that the contract she has inherited is worthless, since Tap hasn't played together for years. But we were aware of a phenomenon that was taking place in the real world. We noticed that old songs by legacy artists would take on new life when they were used in TV shows or videos that went viral. Kate Bush got a huge boost when her song "Running Up That Hill" was featured in an episode of *Stranger Things*. *The Bear* made an anthem of the thirty-year-old R.E.M. song "Strange Currencies."

Since Tap had become part of the real world, I called Sam Levinson, the creator and writer of the hit HBO show *Euphoria*, to ask him about using a Tap song on his show. He loved the idea but couldn't guarantee that the new season of *Euphoria* would come out in time to pull it off. So we came up with a different way to make it work: have a big name in the music world get caught on an iPhone goofing around and singing a Tap song. The video is put up on social media and it goes viral, which creates renewed interest in Spinal Tap.

Hope then recognizes the opportunity to monetize her inherited contract and essentially compels Tap to reunite. This stirs up old wounds. The band hasn't played together for fifteen years. Nigel and David, friends since childhood, have had a falling-out and are not speaking.

Derek, as usual, is caught in the middle. Marty DiBergi, pressed back into service by Hope, dons his USS OORAL SEA cap and eagerly returns to once again make rock and film history.

Not to be a spoiler-alert guy, but what I can tell you is that the story came into focus when we decided that the film would not be built around a tour but one big final concert. Harry initially suggested that it take place in Las Vegas. But for a number of reasons, New Orleans ultimately won out: Harry has a home there; I'd had good experiences making *LBJ* and *Shock and Awe* there; the city has a storied, magical, and musical history; and the tax breaks were good.

**R**ather than run away from the idea of Spinal Tap as a group of aging, no-longer-svelte rockers, we leaned into it. Nigel, David, and Derek are well aware that they're closer to the end than the beginning. As a fitness trainer played by John Michael Higgins tells them, they're at an age where "the candles are starting to cost more than the cake."

At one point, Chris considered giving Nigel a facelift or dyeing Nigel's hair jet-black. But ultimately, he decided against it. "I was thinking about all the famous people out there who have had work done," he says. "I played with the idea of getting one of those stickers that you tape to the sides of your face and then tie it in the back. To give Nigel what I call the G-Force Face. But I thought, 'Boy, that's hard to look at.' We discussed all those possibilities and came down on the side of, even if they wanted face lifts, given their financial situations, they couldn't afford them."

Only David hangs on to the past, with hair mysteriously as long and blond as it was in 1972. Nigel's is now salt-and-pepper, while Derek's is snowy white—this despite the fact that Harry is the only one of us who still has some color left in his real hair.

Harry, by the way, takes pride in the fact that Derek's mustache has always been real. All he needs is eight weeks' lead time to grow out his facial hair. Then, right before we start shooting, he shaves off everything but Derek's walrus mustache. He had the same commitment to Folksmen bassist Mark Shubb's look in *A Mighty Wind*, shaving his head bald and carefully sculpting the thin collar of beard below his chin. Explains Harry, "That kind of beard is called a Newgate fringe. Newgate was a prison in Victorian London, where a lot of the inmates were hanged. The beard is so named because its shape resembles a hangman's noose."

As best we could, we tried to be faithful to the real timeline of Spinal Tap's musical journey as reflected by the band's reunions since we made the first film. At Lucasfilm, there is a battalion of staffers who rigorously maintain the continuity of the *Star Wars* saga, determining what is and isn't "canon." Tap is almost as meticulous. We have a shoebox of memorabilia at the bottom of Michael McKean's closet.

The 1992, 2001, and 2009 tours are where Tap's fictitious lives intersect with the real world. David, Nigel, and Derek really did play Glastonbury, Wembley Stadium, and the Royal Albert Hall. In the sequel, I've worked in footage from those shows, as well as footage from the first film. But we can't deny that keeping all this timeline stuff straight has been a bit of a challenge.

"We have definitely done our share of retrofitting as we've thought this all out," says Michael. "Like, the B-side of '(Listen to the) Flower People' is 'Rainy Day Sun,' which very prominently features keyboards on it. Those have to have been played by someone. That someone, we have determined, is Denny Upham, their keyboardist at the time."

"Not to be confused," adds Chris, "with Ross MacLochness. He's the one who left the band and moved to Namibia. And then released a solo album called *Doesn't Anybody Here Speak English?*"

For the sequel, we brought back David's girlfriend, Jeanine Pettibone; their former record promoter, Artie Fufkin; and their former publicist, Bobbi Flekman. We also brought in two new brilliant improvisers: Kerry Godliman as Hope Faith and Chris Addison as the British promoter Simon Howler.

Paul McCartney makes a special appearance that's based on a real incident. Years ago, while getting ready for their Unwigged tour,

Michael, Chris, and Harry were practicing in a studio at a big rehearsal complex. McCartney happened to be rehearsing with his band in the same complex. One day, Paul poked his head in to say hello.

"He put us on the spot, saying, 'What are you going to play for me, boys?'" says Michael. Once they got past being stunned, the three guys, playing their acoustic instruments, went into the Folksmen's bluegrass version of the Rolling Stones' "Start Me Up." It was the mildest, most sexless version of the song ever performed, even when Michael sang, "You make a dead man come."

When we decided to make the film in New Orleans, we hit upon the idea that, while Tap is rehearsing for their reunion show at the 10,000-seat Lakefront Arena, Paul's in town for his concert at the 80,000-seat Superdome.

To our eternal gratitude, Sir Paul agreed to join us. What we discovered is, on top of all the talents for which he is justly celebrated, the man is a born schnadler. So, too, is a fellow guest performer in the sequel and Knight of the British Empire, Sir Elton John.

Unlike the first time around, for the sequel, we had enough money not to skimp on extras for the concert sequence. We actually had thousands in the crowd cheering Tap on.

Life imitates art. Like the guys in Tap, Chris, Michael, and Harry hadn't played together for fifteen years. But by the time we shot the concert stuff, they had become tight and kicked ass. The crowd was was totally into it. This wasn't a jaded group of Hollywood extras pretending to be enthusiastic—they were genuinely, raucously cheering for Tap, and the guys fed off of them.

"It still is energizing like nothing else that we do," says Chris. "We all do different things outside of Spinal Tap, but there is nothing more fun than walking onto a stage and getting to play music."

"All of our wives were there," recalls Michael, "and it was like we were playing for our own personal girlfriends. There's an expression in stage acting called 'girlfriend level.' Let's say two guys have a fight scene. In rehearsals, you don't go up to girlfriend level. But for a show, one of the guys might say to the other, 'My girlfriend's out there tonight. It'll be intense. I might get a little rough with you.' That day, we were playing at girlfriend level."

It was a beautiful moment. But hey, let's not get too sentimental. This is Spinal Tap we're talking about. Something had to go wrong. When you see the film, you'll find out what it was.

CHAPTER 16

# The Looser the Waistband

In retrospect, calling our 1980 demo reel *Spinal Tap: The Final Tour* was—what's the opposite of prescient? How about "could not be more wrong"?

But this time, does the title fit? Of course, you never say never. But let's face it, we're all getting closer to being reaped by somebody or something grim.

So if this is indeed Tap's last hurrah—the movie, this book, the new album the guys recorded in the summer of '24—well, it has all been, as the saying goes, a lot better than a poke in the eye with a sharp stick.

The making of *This Is Spinal Tap* was one of the greatest experiences of my life. There was nothing better than being creatively connected to friends and getting to make the film we all envisioned.

When I think about it, when we first started dreaming up a movie about a fictitious rock band, Chris, Michael, Harry, and I were a bit like the boys in a film I would make a few years later, *Stand by Me*:

four individuals who embark on an adventure that will forever bond them and change their lives.

We have continued to work together in various combinations. Chris appeared as Count Rugen, the six-fingered man, in *The Princess Bride*, and played a doctor in another film of mine, *A Few Good Men*. Michael and Harry have performed in Chris's brilliant films using the schnadling techniques we originated in *This Is Spinal Tap*.

And everywhere we look, we see the influence of the movie we struggled to get made. You can't scroll through Netflix's or Hulu's home page without stumbling upon a mockumentary TV show, whether it's *The Office, Parks and Recreation, Modern Family, What We Do in the Shadows, Reno 911!, Abbott Elementary,* or *Cunk on Earth*. On IMDb, the most widely trafficked of film-reference websites, ours is the only movie to be rated on a scale of one to eleven.

We were recently asked the question "In what sentence of your obituary do you think *This Is Spinal Tap* will appear?" Here's what we said:

> **CHRIS,** *confidently*: Fourth.
>
> **MICHAEL:** What the fuck?
>
> **HARRY:** First. But it'll share space with *The Simpsons*.
>
> **ROB:** Mine will be "Meathead kicks the bucket." Then maybe *Tap* in the second or third sentence.
>
> **MICHAEL:** What what do I know? As the old joke goes, surprise me.

As you can see, we're a bit uncomfortable talking about legacy. Pomposity is the enemy of satire.

But David St. Hubbins, Nigel Tufnel, and Derek Smalls would have no problem with legacy talk. They live for the pompous. In a new Tap song, "Rockin' in the Urn," written by Harry, Tap waxes poetically on the subject of the beyond. I'll leave you now with an excerpt from Spinal Tap's take on the afterlife:

*It's getting near, the final end*
*Sez a neighbor, sez a friend*

*But as I take my final leave*
*Don't protest, do not grieve*

*Here's my pledge*
*Soon as I burn*
*I'm gonna be rockin' in the urn*

*I've had a kick-ass kind of life*
*Lots of gigs, more than one wife*

*Parties that went on well past dawn*
*House and pool, splendid lawn*

*I'm sad to think*
*I won't return*
*You can bet I'm rockin' in the urn*

*One thing I know about the great hereafter*
*I'll still be blitzing eardrums on the highest rafter*
*You think I was hot at our legendary bashes?*
*Wait 'til you see me when I'm all ashes!*

*I'm gonna be rockin'*
*Rolling and rockin'*
*Gonna be rockin' in the urn*

The end is never the end. The end just continues.

# Acknowledgments

First, we want to thank our wives, who have all come to accept that from time to time, we're compelled to act like silly boys. In ascending ordering of marital longevity: Annette O'Toole (Michael's wife of twenty-five years), Judith Owen (Harry's wife of thirty years), Michele Reiner (Rob's wife of thirty-five years), and the longevity prize goes to Chris Guest and Jamie Lee Curtis (Christopher's wife of forty years and counting). To our parents, Carl and Estelle (Rob), Peter and Jean (Chris), Mack and Dora (Harry), and Gilbert and Ruth (Michael), we want to thank all of you for having the good sense to engage in sexual intercourse and produce four relatively sane children who share a common and twisted sensibility. We'd also like to thank our children, Annie and Ruby; Fletcher, Colin, Nell, and Anna; and Jake, Nick, and Romy, and apologize for any neuroses we may have passed on to you.

*Spinal Tap* would never have been born without its mother, Karen Murphy, who painfully labored to give birth to this admittedly difficult child.

We also want to give a big thanks to all the crew members who helped bring these improbable Tap films to life.

A special shout-out to Aimée Bell, David Kamp, Jennifer Bergstrom, Sally Marvin, and all the folks at Gallery Books and Simon & Schuster who helped realize this book.

And thanks to all the Tap fans, who, over the years, got us, kept us in the zeitgeist, and accepted a modicum of hearing loss.

And finally, to those who are no longer with us: Tony Hendra ("It's not a big college town."); Howard Hesseman ("We have to sit in the lobby and wait for the limo"); Paul Benedict ("I'm just as God made me, sir"); Fred Willard ("Better not get too close, they'll think I'm with the band"); Bruno Kirby ("Frank calls the shots for all these guys"); Ric Parnell ("If I can have the sex and drugs, I can do without the rock 'n' roll"), and Patrick Macnee ("Tap into America"). We miss you and hope to see you in rock 'n' roll heaven, where we hear they have a hell of a band.

THE ISLINGTON PHILHARMONIC ORCHESTRA

PRESENTS

# NIGEL TUFNEL'S

## LICK MY LOVE PUMP

in D Minor

*The Saddest of All Keys*

Lick My Love Pump by Nigel Tufnel ™